First World War
and Army of Occupation
War Diary
France, Belgium and Germany

41 DIVISION
124 Infantry Brigade
King's Royal Rifle Corps
21st Battalion
5 May 1916 - 31 October 1917

WO95/2643/4

The Naval & Military Press Ltd
www.nmarchive.com
Published in association with The National Archives

Published by

The Naval & Military Press Ltd

Unit 10 Ridgewood Industrial Park,

Uckfield, East Sussex,

TN22 5QE England

Tel: +44 (0) 1825 749494

www.naval-military-press.com

www.nmarchive.com

This diary has been reprinted in facsimile from the original. Any imperfections are inevitably reproduced and the quality may fall short of modern type and cartographic standards.

© **Crown Copyright**
Images reproduced by permission of The National Archives, London, England, 2015.

Contents

Document type	Place/Title	Date From	Date To
Miscellaneous	WO95/2643 (4)		
Heading	41st Division 124th Infy Bde 21st Bn K.R.R. Corps May 1916-1917 Oct In Italy 1917 Nov-1918 Mar Disbanded		
Heading	War Diary of 21st Bn King Royal Rifles (German Major) From May 5th To May 31st 1916		
War Diary	Aldershot	05/05/1916	06/05/1916
War Diary	Havre	07/05/1916	07/05/1916
War Diary	Steenbecque	08/05/1916	08/05/1916
War Diary	Renescure	09/05/1916	09/05/1916
War Diary	Outersteene	10/05/1916	30/05/1916
War Diary	La Creche Area	31/05/1916	31/05/1916
Operation(al) Order(s)	Appendix I 21st K.R.R.C. Order No. 1		
Operation(al) Order(s)	Appendix II 21st K.R.R.C. Order No. 2		
Heading	War Diary 21st Bn Kings Royal Rifles (Yeoman Rifles) From June 1 to 1 June 30th 1916 Vol 2		
War Diary	Creslow	01/06/1916	11/06/1916
War Diary	Creslow	12/05/1916	16/05/1916
War Diary	Ploegsteert Wood	17/06/1916	30/06/1916
War Diary	Creslow	30/06/1916	30/06/1916
Heading	War Diary 21st Battn Kings Royal Rifles (Yeoman Rifles) July 1st to July 31st 1916		
War Diary	Ploegsteert Wood	01/07/1916	11/07/1916
War Diary	Papot	11/07/1916	17/07/1916
War Diary	Ploegsteert Wood	17/07/1916	27/07/1916
War Diary	Creslow Ploegsteert Wood (Hunterston)	23/07/1916	27/07/1916
War Diary	Ploegsteert Wood	27/07/1917	31/07/1917
War Diary	Ploegsteert Wood	28/07/1916	29/07/1916
Miscellaneous	From Officer Commanding 21st K.R.R.C. To Headquarters 124th Infantry Brigade.		
Heading	War Diary 21st Battn Kings Royal Rifles (Yeoman Rifles) August 1st to August 31st 1916 Vol 4		
War Diary	Ploegsteert Wood	01/08/1916	03/08/1916
War Diary	Papot	03/08/1916	08/08/1916
War Diary	Ploegsteert Wood	09/08/1916	17/08/1916
War Diary	Papot	17/08/1916	17/08/1916
War Diary	Meteren	18/08/1916	18/08/1916
War Diary	Bailleul	23/08/1916	23/08/1916
War Diary	Pont Remy	24/08/1916	24/08/1916
War Diary	Francieres	24/08/1916	24/08/1916
War Diary	Bailleul W. Stn Pont Remy	23/08/1916	24/08/1916
War Diary	Francieres	24/08/1916	31/08/1916
Heading	War Diary 21st Battn Kings Royal Rifles (Yeoman Rifles) September 1st to September 30th 1916 Vol 5		
War Diary	Francieres	01/09/1916	06/09/1916
War Diary	Long Pre	07/09/1916	07/09/1916
War Diary	Dernancourt	08/09/1916	13/09/1916
War Diary	Pomieres	14/09/1916	14/09/1916
War Diary	Delville Wood	15/09/1916	17/09/1916
War Diary	Dernancourt Wood	16/09/1916	30/09/1916

War Diary	War Diary 21st Battn Kings Royal Rifles (Yeoman Rifles) Oct 1st to October 31st 1916 Vol 6		
War Diary	Dernancourt	02/10/1916	02/10/1916
War Diary	Tommiers Redoubt	01/10/1916	01/10/1916
War Diary	Wood Lane	03/10/1916	05/10/1916
War Diary	Flers Trench	05/10/1916	06/10/1916
War Diary	Gird Trench	06/10/1916	08/10/1916
War Diary	Gird Support	08/10/1916	10/10/1916
War Diary	Fricourt	11/10/1916	11/10/1916
War Diary	Becordel	12/10/1916	12/10/1916
War Diary	Buire	13/10/1916	16/10/1916
War Diary	Airaines	16/10/1916	17/10/1916
War Diary	Allery	17/10/1916	20/10/1916
War Diary	Meteren	20/10/1916	20/10/1916
War Diary	Victoria Camp	21/10/1916	21/10/1916
War Diary	Trenches In Bois Carre Area.	22/10/1916	28/10/1916
War Diary	La Clytte	29/10/1916	31/10/1916
Miscellaneous	Nominal Roll		
Heading	Vol 8. 21st Bn. K.R.R.C. 2-12-16 to 31-12-16		
Heading	War Diary 21st Battn Kings Royal Rifles (Yeoman Rifles) Dec 1st to Dec 31st 1916 Vol 8		
War Diary	Ridgewood.	02/12/1916	07/12/1916
War Diary	In The Line	08/12/1916	13/12/1916
War Diary	La Llytte	13/12/1916	14/12/1916
War Diary	Ridgewood.	02/12/1916	07/12/1916
War Diary		03/12/1916	03/12/1916
War Diary	The Line	08/12/1916	13/12/1916
War Diary	La Llytte	13/12/1916	25/12/1916
War Diary	La Llytte.	14/12/1916	25/12/1916
War Diary	Ridgewood.	27/12/1916	31/12/1916
Miscellaneous	21st Battalion The King's The King' Royal Rifle Corps (Yeoman Rifles) Appendix	01/12/1916	01/12/1916
Miscellaneous	21st Battalion The King's King' Royal Rifle Corps (Yeoman Rifles) Appendix	01/12/1916	01/12/1916
Miscellaneous	21st Battalion The King's King' Royal Rifle Corps (Yeoman Rifles) Appendix.	01/12/1916	01/12/1916
Heading	War Diary 21st Battn Kings Royal Rifles (Yeoman Rifles) January 1st to January 31st 1916. Vol 9		
War Diary	Ridge Wood	02/01/1917	02/01/1917
War Diary	In The Line	06/01/1917	08/01/1917
War Diary	La Llytte	09/01/1917	14/01/1917
War Diary	In The Line	20/01/1917	20/01/1917
War Diary	Ridge Wood	20/01/1919	31/01/1917
War Diary	The Line	01/02/1917	01/02/1917
War Diary	La Llytte	05/02/1917	05/02/1917
War Diary	The Line	10/02/1917	10/02/1917
War Diary	Ridge Wood	16/02/1917	16/02/1917
War Diary	The Line	17/02/1917	17/02/1917
War Diary	The Line	16/02/1917	22/02/1917
War Diary	Chippewa Camp	24/02/1917	28/02/1917
War Diary	The Line	01/03/1917	06/03/1917
War Diary	Ridge Wood	06/03/1917	06/03/1917
War Diary	The Line	12/03/1917	18/03/1917
War Diary	La Clytte	18/03/1917	18/03/1917
War Diary	Steenvoorde	21/03/1917	31/03/1917
Map	Quarante to Canal.		

Map	German Lines From Bois		
Heading	War Diary 21st Battn Kings Royal Rifles (Yeoman Rifles) April 1st to April 30th 1916 Vol 12		
War Diary	Steenvoorde	01/04/1917	05/04/1917
War Diary	Dickebusch	06/04/1917	30/04/1917
Heading	War Diary 21st Battn Kings Royal Rifles (Yeoman Rifles) 1st May To 31st May 1917 Vol 13		
War Diary	Micmac & Dickebusch	01/05/1917	03/05/1917
War Diary	Alberta Reninghelst	04/05/1917	16/05/1917
War Diary	G21. A.2.7 Sheet 27.	17/05/1917	17/05/1917
War Diary	Eperlecques	18/05/1917	31/05/1917
Map	41st Divisional Front.		
War Diary	Meteren	17/07/1917	18/07/1917
War Diary	Westoutre	19/07/1917	30/07/1917
War Diary	Ref Map	30/07/1917	30/07/1917
War Diary	Zillebeke Sheet 28 NW 4 Sheet 28 NE 3	31/07/1917	31/07/1917
Miscellaneous	Yeoman Rifles Operation Order No. 29 by Lieut-Col. Talbot McL. Jarvis. D.S.O. Appendix I	26/07/1917	26/07/1917
War Diary		01/08/1917	07/08/1917
War Diary	Scottish Wood	08/08/1917	09/08/1917
War Diary	H 35.c. Central	09/08/1917	15/08/1917
War Diary	Thieshouck	15/08/1917	18/08/1917
Operation(al) Order(s)	Appendix X	28/08/1917	28/08/1917
War Diary	Thieshouck	18/08/1917	25/08/1917
War Diary	Le Nieppe	26/08/1917	27/08/1917
War Diary	Tatinghem	27/08/1917	31/08/1917
Heading	21st Bn. Kings Royal Rifle Corps (Yeoman Rifles) War Diary 1st Sept 1917 to 31st Sept. 1917 Vol 17		
War Diary	Tatinghem	01/09/1917	14/09/1917
War Diary	Oxelaere	15/09/1917	16/09/1917
War Diary	Ridge Wood	17/09/1917	18/09/1917
War Diary	Shrewsbury Forest	19/09/1917	23/09/1917
War Diary	Le Peuplier	24/09/1917	30/09/1917
Miscellaneous	To Officer Commanding.	30/09/1917	30/09/1917
Heading	21st Battalion Kings Royal Rifle Corps (Yeoman Rifles) War Diary 1st Oct 1917 to 31st Oct 1917 Vol 18		
War Diary	Ghyvelde	01/10/1917	06/10/1917
War Diary	La Panne	06/10/1917	14/10/1917
War Diary	Oost Dunkerke Bains	15/10/1917	29/10/1917
War Diary	Teteghem	30/10/1917	31/10/1917
Operation(al) Order(s)	124th. Infantry Brigade Operation Order No. 157	04/10/1917	04/10/1917
Miscellaneous			
Miscellaneous	Administrative Instructions Reference 124th. Infantry Brigade Order No. 137	05/10/1917	05/10/1917
Miscellaneous	Officer Commanding.	05/10/1917	05/10/1917
Miscellaneous	Location Of Units 41st Division.		
Operation(al) Order(s)	Operation Order No. 64 by Major G.L Brown. Commanding 21st Battalion King's Royal Rifle Corps. Friday 5th October 1917 Appendix I	05/10/1917	05/10/1917
Miscellaneous			
Operation(al) Order(s)	124th. Infantry Brigade Operation Order No. 138	12/10/1917	12/10/1917
Miscellaneous			
Miscellaneous	To Officer Commanding.	12/10/1917	12/10/1917
Miscellaneous	Amendment To 124th. Infantry Brigade Operation Order No. 138	13/10/1917	13/10/1917

Operation(al) Order(s)	Operation Order No. 65 by Lieut.-Col. G. L. Brown. Commanding 21st Battalion King's Royal Rifle Corp. Appendix II	13/10/1917	13/10/1917
Miscellaneous	Distribution		
Miscellaneous	Officer Commanding.	14/10/1917	14/10/1917
Operation(al) Order(s)	Operation Order No. 66 by Lieut.-Col. G. L. Brown Commanding 21st Battalion King's Royal Rifle Corps. Appendix III	21/10/1917	21/10/1917
Operation(al) Order(s)	124th. Infantry Brigade Order No. 139	22/10/1917	22/10/1917
Operation(al) Order(s)	Addenda to Operation Order No. 66	22/10/1917	22/10/1917
Operation(al) Order(s)	124th. Infantry Brigade Order No. 141	28/10/1917	28/10/1917
Operation(al) Order(s)	Operation Order No. 67 by lieut. Col. G. L. Brown Commanding 21st Battalion King's Royal Rifle Corps. Appendix IV	28/10/1917	28/10/1917
Miscellaneous	124th Inf Bde		

W005/26434(4)

W005/26043(4)

41ST DIVISION
124TH INFY BDE

21ST BN K.R.R.CORPS

MAY 1916 — 1917 OCT

IN ITALY 1917 NOV — 1918 MAR

DISBANDED

ant.

WAR DIARY
or
INTELLIGENCE SUMMARY

Confidential

War Diary
of
21st Bn. King's Royal Rifles (Yeoman Rifles)

From May 5th to May 31st 1916.

WAR DIARY
or
INTELLIGENCE SUMMARY
(Erase heading not required.)

Army Form C. 2118.

Place	Date	Hour	Summary of Events and Information	Remarks and references to Appendices
Aldershot	5-5-16	12.15am	The Battalion left Aldershot and entrained at FARNBOROUGH STATION (2 trains) for SOUTHAMPTON.	
"		7.1.m	Entrained left SOUTHAMPTON by S.S. Mosquito. 10 Officers also on board.	
HAVRE	6.5.16	7.30am	Disembarked at HAVRE. Marched to rest camp.	
"	7.5.16	11.0pm	Entrained One D. Coy in late train	
STEENBECQUE	8.5.16	10.30am	Detrained. One D. Coy. Marched to B. Coy. joined later by "B" Coy.	
RENESCURE	10-5-16	9.00am	Marched to OUTERSTEENE being Billetted by the 124th Brigade. Inspected on the march near HAZEBROUCK by G.O.C. II Army and G.O.C. II Corps. Arrived at 6.30 pm and went into billets.	

WAR DIARY or INTELLIGENCE SUMMARY

Army Form C. 2118.

Place	Date	Hour	Summary of Events and Information	Remarks and references to Appendices
OUTERSTEENE	10th		The Bn. Signallers went by motor lorry to the trenches for instruction, and remained till the 20th.	
"	11th		Demonstration of anti-gas measures.	
"	15th-17th		Parties of officers N.C.O's + men were attached during these days to Battalions in the trenches for instruction. The C.O. and Adjutant were attached to the 8th Seaforth Watch from 16th - 18th, other parties were also attached to the same battalion and to the 11th Royal Scots. The remainder of the Battalion continued training.	
"	26th		Inspection of the Battalion by G.O.C. Brigade Genl. CLEMSON.	

2/5-16

Army Form C. 2118.

WAR DIARY
or
INTELLIGENCE SUMMARY

(Erase heading not required.)

Instructions regarding War Diaries and Intelligence Summaries are contained in F. S. Regs., Part II. and the Staff Manual respectively. Title Pages will be prepared in manuscript.

Place	Date	Hour	Summary of Events and Information	Remarks and references to Appendices
OUTERSTEENE	May 1916 30th	6.15 p.m.	Moved & billetted in La Crèche area. Billetted at F.12.a.3.3 (Sheet 36 A) 1/40,000	Orders Appendix 1
LA CRÈCHE area	31st	3 a.m.	Marched to CRESLOW & take up Reserve billets in rear of 122nd Brigade Hd Qrs at U.25.a.8.8 (Sheet 28 1/40,000) about 800 yds N of PLOEGSTEERT village. Battalion two platoons W end of PLOEGSTEERT wood. 2 platoons at TOUQUET BERTHE FARM	" 2

1-6-16

Furnham
LIEUT.-COL.
KING'S ROYAL RIFLES,
COMMANDING. 21st BATTN.
(YEOMAN RIFLES.)

Appendix I.

21st K.R.R.C. Order No 1.   Copy No II

1. The Bn will move into Billets in La CRECHE area on May 30th 1916.
2. Starting Point 'A' Coy's billets.
3. Time 6.15 P.M.
4. Route F.4b.5.9.(Sheet 36A) — X 29 b.1.4½ (Sheet 27) SWYNSTAEL — X 30 a.5.4 (Sheet 27) — Level Crossing X 30.C.22 (Sheet 27) — F.6a 5.7 (Sheet 36A) F.12a.3.3 (Sheet 36A).
5. Order of march Hd Qrs. A.B.C.D Coys. A+B. Echelons. 1st line Transport.
6. Position of new Bn Hd Qrs. F.12a 3.3 (sheet 36 A)
7. The Bn billetting Officer + 1. N.C.O per Coy, will meet Coys on arrival at Bn Hd Qrs. + conduct them to their billets.
8. Ref (para 7 atove) 2nd Lt Hervey will collect 1. N.C.O. from each Coy. + 1 from R.S.M (for Hd Qrs + M. Gunners) + proceed to the new Bn Hd Qrs, + make billetting arrangements. This party to arrive at new Hd Qrs at 1. P.M. 30.5.16.
9. All blankets + spare Kits (if any) will be sent to the Q.M's Stores as under. A. Coy. 10. a.m. B.Coy 10.15 a.m. C. Coy 10.30 a.m D.Coy 10.45 a.m. Hd Qrs + Specialists 11.0. a.m.
Blankets will be rolled in bundles of 10 + securely tied at each end + labelled with the Coy's letter (specialists with a distinctive mark). All kits will also be labelled with the Coy. letter.
10. All Officer's Kits of Hd Qrs. B+D Coys will be sent to the Q.M's stores by 3. P.M. + wagons will be sent to collect Officer's Kits of A + C Coys at 2.p.m. The Officer's Kits of the 2 latter Coys. will be stacked outside their Coy. Hds. by that time.

APPENDIX II

21st KRRC Order No 2. Copy No 11 Retained

1. The Battalion will relieve the 8th Bn Black Watch in Reserve Positions at CRESLOW (U.25.a.9.9.) Sheet 28 [1 Coy + 4 Guns]
TOUQET BERTHE (1 Coy) PLUGSTREET WOOD WEST (2 Coys)
Relief to be completed by 6.20am on 31.5.16.

2. Starting Point A.7.a.7.8 (Road Junction) Sheet 36.

3. Time. A Coy 3.0am – B. Coy. 3.5am – C Coy 3.10am – D Coy. 3.15am.
Snipers, Head Qrs, and Machine Gunners 3.20am.

4. Route. Railway Crossing (S.27.a.7.0) Sheet 28. – PONT D'ACHELLES (Sheet 36) – LE ROMARIN (Sheet 36) by field track from LE ROMARIN. Guides from 8th Black Watch will meet Platoons at LE ROMARIN.

5. The Battalion will march by Coys until turning EAST of the BAILLEUL-NIEPPE ROAD (PONT D'ACHELLES) Map 28. From this point by Platoons at 200 yards distance.

6. Companies will report immediately relief of their Coys is completed.

7. 2nd Lieut. Back. will collect 1 NCO from each Coy + 1 from 4 Qrs (to be detailed by RSM) to form an advanced Party. This Party will arrive at LE ROMARIN (road junction R.1.a.6.3) at 6pm 30.5.16 where they will be met by guides.

8. Re: Para 5 of these orders: Lieut Beardown will be in Command of the Snipers – 4 Qrs – and Machine Gun Section + on reaching the Point where troops have to march by Platoons at 200 yards distance, will divide his command up into Parties of about Platoon Strengths. If the Officer or NCO of any Party or Platoon has not the required MAPS + does not know the route he must follow the Platoon in front of him at 200 yards distance by means of connecting files.

9. The transport will pass Starting Point at 3.25am. and go direct to their lines at PAPOT. When the Bn is settled in Billets 6 Cycle orderlies will be sent back to Transport to guide Waggons-Cookers etc to Coys.

10. Wednesdays Breakfast rations will be drawn from RM. at 2pm 30-5-16.
Hot tea will be issued to Coys at 2am 31-5-16. before marching. Dinners will be brought to Coys in Kitchens in Reserve Billet at about 12 noon.

PTO.

2

11. A Coy will be billeted at TOQUET BERTHE
B & C Coys - - - In the Wood at HUNTERS TOWN
D Coy - - - CRESLOW.
Hdrs - - - CRESLOW.

12. The Maltese Cart will go with Head Quarters under Lieut Sheardown

Army Form C. 2118.

WAR DIARY
or
INTELLIGENCE SUMMARY
(Erase heading not required.)

21. K.R.R.C

Vol 2

June

Confidential

War Diary

21st Bn. Kings Royal Rifles (Yeoman Rifles)

from June 1st to June 30th 1916.

Army Form C. 2118.

WAR DIARY
or
INTELLIGENCE SUMMARY

(Erase heading not required.)

Instructions regarding War Diaries and Intelligence Summaries are contained in F. S. Regs., Part II. and the Staff Manual respectively. Title Pages will be prepared in manuscript.

Place	Date	Hour	Summary of Events and Information	Remarks and references to Appendices
Open Lane	1st June to 5th June		The Bn remained in billets, finding working parties to supplement work in the front & support lines, held by the 15th Bn Hampshire Regt. During our period in billets, we had 20 Casualties; 5-3 wounded while working on a Communication Trench, 9-16 in billets in the wood for Caused by Shrapnel, 1 one in wood Caused by a stray rifle bullet. Relieved the 15th Bn Hants Regt. in the front line. Relief commenced 5 A.M. Completed 8.20 A.M.	
	June 5th			
	June 6th		Notification received from 124 Bde. that Bde. & Div. artillery were going to bombard a hostile work at U.28.a 4.6 sheet 28. This work is opposite Trench 110 Held by the 10th Bn Queens R.W.S. Regt. A Coy holding Trenches 113 & 114 had orders to work hard to support him during the bombardment. The enemy immediately retaliated by bombarding Trench 120 & CT 119 held by C Coy. This did little damage, Causing only 4 Casualties. our total Casualties during the time we held the Trenches [113 - 120] were 9 wounded and 3 killed Dispositions while in the Trenches. No 1 Platoon sans Trench S2 113 No 2 " No 3 " Trench T 113 No 4 " " S1. 113	

2449 Wt. W14957/M90 750,000 1/16 J.B.C. & A. Forms/C.2118/12.

Army Form C. 2118.

WAR DIARY
or
INTELLIGENCE SUMMARY
(Erase heading not required.)

Instructions regarding War Diaries and Intelligence Summaries are contained in F. S. Regs., Part II. and the Staff Manual respectively. Title Pages will be prepared in manuscript.

Place	Date	Hour	Summary of Events and Information	Remarks and references to Appendices
"			No 5 Platoon Trench S2.116 " 6 " " Trench loop ET117 & ET116 " 7 " " Trench T 116 " 8 " " " T 117 " 9 " " " T 119 " 10 " " " T 118 " 11 " " " T 120 " 12 " " " S 120 " 13 " " EELES FORT (HUNTERS AVENUE) " 14 " " READING FORT " " " 15 " " REGENT FORT " " " 16 " " EEL PIE FORT " " Trenches T114 & T115 were undefended. This Gap was named Gap G.	orders Appendix 3
"	June 11th		Relieved by 15th & 13th Hants Regt. & returned to previous billets. Relief commenced 5 AM. Completed 7.20 am. orders appendix 3 attached.	

D.D. Trumpeldor asgdt
for
LIEUT-COL
KING'S ROYAL RIFLES,
COMNDING. 21st BATTN.
(YEOMAN RIFLES.)

WAR DIARY or INTELLIGENCE SUMMARY

Army Form C. 2118.

Place	Date	Hour	Summary of Events and Information	Remarks and references to Appendices
CRESSION	June 12th/16		The Bn. remained in rest billets, finding working parties for work in front & support lines, held by the 15th Bn HAMPSHIRE REGT. Bathing parties went to PONT DE NIEPPE.	
PLOEGSTEERT WOOD		17th	The Bn. relieved the 15th Batt: HAMPSHIRE REGT. at 5 A.M. Relief completed 7.40 A.M. There was relief was on this, and the following day, on orders from Brigade.	
		18th/19th	During the night a Gas Alarm was taken up, but no gas noticed in the Trenches.	
		19th	The 32nd Bn ROYAL FUSILIERS discharged 100 Smoke Bombs & lit 50 PAYNE's Smoke Candles between 5.0 p.m. & 5.4 p.m., T.123. The enemy's artillery retaliated from 5.10 p.m. with shrapnel from 5.2 p.m. to 5.4 p.m. Enemy artillery reserve briny & forming a to 5.30 p.m. shelling PALK VILLA on support reserve briny & forming a barrage at HUNTERS AVENUE. No one was hit, but a short piece of rail was torn up on NORTH BRITISH RLY. in tram of EEL PIE FORT.	
		20.	Smoke operation repeated — by 10th Bn QUEENS — T. 108/110. from 6 p.m. to 6.4 p.m. Our artillery commenced bombardment of enemy front line at 6.12 p.m. The enemy's retaliation was insignificant.	
		21.	This Bn: repeated the Smoke operation — T. 112/114 — from 5.30 p.m. to 5.34 p.m. On artillery bombarding enemy's front line from 5.32 to 5.34 p.m. Enemy did not retaliate.	
		22.	The 123rd BRIGADE carr. smoke from T. 101/2 at 3 p.m. This Bn. not affected. On the night of 22/23. GAS ALARM taken up & our artillery bombarded enemy front line. NO GAS noticed in Trenches held by this Bn.	

Army Form C. 2118.

WAR DIARY
or
INTELLIGENCE SUMMARY
(Erase heading not required.)

Place	Date 1916	Hour	Summary of Events and Information	Remarks and references to Appendices
PLOEGSTEERT WOOD	June	24	Disposition while in the Trenches	
			As during preceding tour of duty, excepting A. Coy. holding HUNTERS AVENUE Forts in place of D. Coy. holding T.113, S.T.1.113, S.T.2.113. T.114, 115 (GAP 97 was undefended. Relieved by 1/5th HANTS & returned to previous billets. Relief commenced 5. A.M. – all Companies back in billets 8.10 A.M.	orders Appendix 4, attached
			Our total casualties during period we held the Trenches [113-120] 17th to 24th June, were: 5 killed 4 wounded.	
	24/30		The Bn. remained in reserve billets (PLOEGSTEERT WOOD, CRESLOW (H.Q.) & TOUQUET BERTHE), finding working parties to work in front and support lines, under R.E. supervision. Reserve billets were made strong, and a Fort commenced in the reserve billets' area.	
	30		Our artillery bombarded the enemy's line during the day and the Batt" remained near its usual positions in readiness for retaliation. From 10 p.m. until 12.30 midnight our artillery bombarded followed up by a raid heavily, and gas was sent over. The enemy's line by N2 & 15 Bn.	
			HANTS: The enemy retaliated on our front line, supports, & reserve	

WAR DIARY
or
INTELLIGENCE SUMMARY

Army Form C. 2118.

Place	Date	Hour	Summary of Events and Information	Remarks and references to Appendices
CRESLOW	1916 June 30		Nowe killed: the Batt: remained in its strong position, - the Barricade (between lines BUNHILL ROW & junction of WARNER AV. & REGENT St. to TOUQUET BERTH(E), and blockhouses in HUNTERSTON - until normal conditions were resumed. During this bombardment we had two men killed and four wounded (two being stretcher bearers, not interfering with effectiveness) in looking after the well we had to have wounded. A stretcher bearer was evacuated during the week owing to wounds.	

Fordham
LIEUT-COL
KING'S ROYAL RIFLES,
COMMDING. 21ST BATTN.
(YEOMAN RIFLES.)

Army Form C. 2118.

WAR DIARY
or
INTELLIGENCE SUMMARY
(Erase heading not required.)

41/ 21.K.R.R.C Vol 3

Confidential

War Diary

21st Batt: Kings Royal Rifles (Yeoman Rifles)

July 1st to July 31st 1916.

WAR DIARY or INTELLIGENCE SUMMARY

Place	Date 1916	Hour	Summary of Events and Information	Remarks and references to Appendices
Ploegsteert Wood	1st July	5 a.m.	The Battn. relieved the 15th Bn. HANTS in the front line. Relief commenced 5 a.m., completed 8.30 a.m.	
"	9th "		At 11.30 p.m. a minor enterprise was carried out by the 32nd Batt. ROYAL FUSILIERS on our left, to the front line of capturing prisoners & bombing at most known no provide to the enemy. Hostile retaliation did not affect us. To divert hostile attention, this Battn. was to discharge smoke bombs & wind permits, when testing direction strength of wind, the trial bombs went off premature, severely burning Lieut. G. BURTON & C.S.M. GIBSON — both evacuated. Battn. relieved by 10th Battn. "THE QUEENS" R.W. SURREY REGT. Relief commenced 5 a.m., completed 7.25 a.m. We marched to rest billets at PAPOT. During the tour of duty in the Trenches, were carried out in accordance with Schedule. Own casualties were: 3 men killed, 1 Officer wounded, 13 NCO's & men wounded — of whom 3 were not evacuated.	
"	11th "		Minor Enterprise. During the night of July 10/11, a minor enterprise was carried out by this Battn. against hostile trenches opposite T.113. Party consisted of 1 Officer [2nd Lt. R.W. LAW] 7 NCOs & 26 Riflemen. Special Report is attached. Whilst in rest billets, no dispositions were changed — A.Coy. occupying T.115/4/7 instead of B.Coy., which occupied HUNTERS AVENUE. D.Coy. again held T.113/4. at " Coy T. 118/9/120.	

WAR DIARY or INTELLIGENCE SUMMARY

Army Form C. 2118.

Place	Date	Hour	Summary of Events and Information	Remarks and references to Appendices
PAPOT	July 1/17		Battn. remained in rest billets at PAPOT, furnishing working parties. But 7 working parties RE & Special RE, commencing night of 11/12.	
PLOEGSTEERT WOOD		17	Battn. marched from Papot to relieve 10th Bn. "Queens" R.W.S. Regt. Relief commenced 5 A.m. Completed 8.40 A.m. D.Coy. held T.113-114 (GHQ2), A.Coy. T.115 (G4G) -117, B.Coy. T.118-120, C.Coy. Hunters Avenue (S.end to the STRAND).	
		18	9.15 p.m. to 11.15 p.m. Artillery fire against hostile roads & communications. Morning fired; wire cutting by an artillery off. G.A.T.F. 9 T. 113.	
		19	Morning fired: repetition of previous morning.	
		20	A surprise gas attack with smoke discharges had been arranged to take place between 12 midnight & 3 A.m. (20/21) but was cancelled.	
	2/2/23		A raid was to have been made by one Coy. 12th Bn.(?) B? & 1 Coy.12/23 Inf. Bgd during the night against hostile front line trenches from U.22.C.4.2 to U.28.a.3½.8. (Map ST.YVES. 1/10,000, part of 17a.28) against RED HOUSE locality repeating but was postponed.	
		23	The B.t was relieved by 10th Bn. "Queen" R.W.S. Rgt. by 7.0 A.m. & took own reserve billets at CRESLOW from 26 Bn. ROYAL FUSILIERS, excepting C.Coy. which remained in HUNTERS AVENUE	

WAR DIARY or INTELLIGENCE SUMMARY

Army Form C. 2118.

Place	Date	Hour	Summary of Events and Information	Remarks and references to Appendices
PLOEGSTEERT WOOD	July 23/		AVENUE until July 27ᵗʰ, when it was relieved early in the morning by D.Coy.	
	27/		To Battⁿ. In the evening C.Coy. relieved HUNTERS AVENUE. D. going to T.113, 14 Battⁿ. re-entering the line on this day, in the Trenches 17/ 23ʳᵈ July. Our casualties during tour of duty were: WOUNDED & EVACUATED 13 KILLED 8.	
CRESLOW & PLOEGSTEERT WOOD (HUNTERSTON)	23/27		The Battⁿ. less One Company – remained in Reserve Billets, finding working parties to various R.E. H.Q. at CRESLOW. A.Coy. in HUNTERSTON South, D.Coy. HUNTERSTON North, B.Coy at TOUQUET BERTHE FARM.	
	26/27		Raid on enemy line opposite G.A.F. at T.113 was carried out on night 26/(27) by a Coy. of 10ᵗʰ Bⁿ. "QUEENS" R.W.S. Reg.ᵗ, accompanied by demolition party R.E. & supported by DIVIS.ˡ ARTILLERY, Stokes Guns etc. Our Batt⁻ went into support positions near its billets, but was not affected by the operations; it remained in readiness to turn out should occasion arise, till orders were received to resume Normal.	
PLOEGSTEERT WOOD	27	2:30pm	This Bⁿ. relieved 10ᵗʰ Bⁿ. "Queens" entered the line on in Right. T.103-111. The 15ᵗʰ Bⁿ. HANTS relieved this Bⁿ. at CRESLOW. One Corp. A. & R.C.H.D	
	30		returned to this unit from prisoners of War line; on July 30, C.Coy. relieved D.Coy. in T.113. D.Coy. entered HUNTERS AVENUE.	
	31.		On casualties from 23/7/16 to 31/7/16 were: Reserve Billets, Killed 1 Wounded 1	

WAR DIARY
or
INTELLIGENCE SUMMARY

Army Form C. 2118.

4

Place	Date	Hour	Summary of Events and Information	Remarks and references to Appendices
PLOEGSTEERT WOOD	July 31		[Casualties (cont)] + in the line: 1 Killed 2 wounded.	
"	28		2nd Lt Knox awarded Military Cross for gallantry and devotion to duty night of 10/11th July.	
"	29		9/12003 Cpl J.H. McGurn awarded the D.C.M. for gallantry + devotion to duty night of 10/11 July.	

Farnham
LIEUT.-COL.
KING'S ROYAL RIFLES,
COMNDING. 21st BATTN.
(YEOMAN RIFLES.)
1.8.16

(1)

15.

D.

From Officer Commanding 21st K.R.R.C.
To Head Quarters 124th Infantry Brigade.

Sir,

I have the honour to report that in accordance with your order No. 25, a minor enterprise, with the intention of capturing prisoners and doing as much damage as possible to the enemy was carried out by this Battalion last night 10/11th July against the hostile trenches opposite Trench 113. Strength of party 1 Officer, 4 N.C.Os. & 26 men. Nominal Roll attached.

<u>Disposition</u>. The party was divided into three groups of 9, numbered X. Y. Z; Each group was further sub-divided into sections of 3, in accordance with orders issued by me, already submitted.

<u>At 11.45 p.m.</u> the party paraded in gap G. Their equipment was carefully checked, it consisted of 4 men with rifles and swords, remainder bombs in bombing waistcoats and knobkerries. N.C.Os. knobkerries and revolvers. 9 men with wire-cutters in addition to arms. 9 men with electric torches, hand and faces were blackened with burnt cork. Steel helmets were not worn, all titles, identity discs and all marks of identification were left behind. 9 men took Scaling-ladders.

<u>12.20 a.m</u>. The first man the leader of the party 2nd Lieut. R.W.R. Law. went over the parapet in bay 7 T.113. The remainder of the party followed in single file, the last man passing over at 12.34 a.m.

<u>12.41 a.m</u>. The signal of one Very-light was fired from Picket House in the direction of the Bardcage. On this signal the party advanced in line of 3s. at about 3 yards. interval creeping through the grass. Our machine gun fire was applied intermittently on the enemy's parapet all the Evening, with a view to preventing the mending of the wire.

2.

12.41.
At this time, our machine guns, increased their fire, in accordance with my instructions, the object being to drown the noise of the party creeping through the grass.
The Artillery bombardment and the signal for the rush into the enemy's trenches was timed for 1.0. am.
The bombardment commenced at 12.59. & was followed half a minute later, by the firing of the signal "2 Very lights from Picket House". This signal was very easily distinguished by the party, who knew exactly from which part to expect them. During the advance through the grass 2nd Lt. Law heard a hostile wiring party in front of him, and at the signal of the two Very lights, the whole party got up and pushed for the trench. They had reached the enemy's wire before being fired at, while they were negotiating the wire, they were greeted with, machine gun, rifle fire & bombs.
C.S.M. McEwen succeeded in getting through the wire rather in front of 2nd Lt. Law, and got on to the enemy's parapet. He was distinctly able to see the enemy's Machine gun emplacement and some Germans in the trench, but at this time he was knocked over by the explosion of a hostile bomb, into a pit full of wire, but escaped injury.
2nd Lt. Law had considerable difficulty with the wire, but emptied his revolver into the enemy. As they went over the parapet into the trench, the remainder of the party attacked vigourously with revolvers, rifle fire and bombs, discharging approximately 110 bombs. They heard a good deal of yelling on the part of the Germans, and are confident that a considerable number of their bombs took effect. One man was on the point of bayoneting a German close to his own parapet when he was wounded and the German escaped. At about 1.6. am. seeing that it was impossible to enter the trench, as the majority of the party were held up by the wire, they gradually withdrew to a ditch, in front of our own wire and laid down in the grass,

and awaited instructions to come in over the parapet. The signals to return were duly given as arranged for at 1.8.a.m. and were observed without difficulty. By 1.45. a.m. the majority of the men had come in. Search parties under 2nd Lt Hervey and Sgt Salmon who both did very useful work, went out of the trenches to look for the remainder and to help with the wounded. By 2.20 a.m. the last man who at first was reported as missing had been brought up.

As previously stated the artillery bombardment commenced at 12.59. a.m. and as far as can be ascertained the accuracy of the shooting was quite satisfactory.

The enemy retaliated very slightly, sending over only one large shell, or possibly Trench-mortar, which fell somewhere near the Support line of T.113

Enemy's Machine-gun Emplacement

C.S.M. McEwen states that the enemy's Machine-gun Emplacement appeared to consist of a concrete platform in front and behind a steel plate with a loophole. He is of opinion that the gun was firing through the loophole, and suggests that the emplacement was so designed that a screen can be easily drawn over it.

Enemy's wire

In spite of some rather narrow gaps having been made in the wire two days previously by the artillery, the party found that the wire confronting them was a considerable obstacle. In addition to Knife-rests which had been demolished in front of the right hand section, there appeared to be ditches full of wire which sank under pressure and were difficult to get out of. There also appeared to be pits and holes full of wire. In some places the wire was a thick tangled mass.

4

General remarks.

Prisoner obtained it be impossible a prisoner
captured up so close to the exit of the party, he could have
been escaped if the boats had been of the same quality as ours.

Conclusions

From the observations of the Officers, N.C.O's & men who
took part in the raid, it appears that undoubtedly a strong
working party was present in the section of the trench attacked,
and it is possible that as there had been a lull in the
Machine Gun fire, between 12.0 & 12.20 the working party
was covered by bombers and had just started to repair the
gaps in the wire. It is not clear whether their retirement to
their own trench was due in the first instance to their having
detected the raiders or to the fact that our Machine gun
fire had again become active. I consider that the raid was
well led and well carried out by all ranks, when faced with
one of the all, above situations which was contemplated in
their orders, they acted in accordance therewith. I would
like to draw your attention to the good work done by the
leaders of the party C.S.M. McEwen, Sgt Campbell, Rfmn.
Statler, Rfmn. Bell & Rfmn. G. H. Curry.

Casualties - 12164 Rfm. BELL. T.W. Died of wounds on by
Sgts Barker & Lehman). - 12564 Rfm. WOOD. W. wounded.
- 12592 Rfm. STABLER. S. wounded. - 12195 Rfm. HOLT. W.
wounded (all in wire). - 12360 Rfm. EMMERSON. G. O.
and - Rfm. FAIL. R (slightly & on duty)

In accordance with G. H. Q. letter 134/15/ G.605 ordering that in minor attempts
an Officer should be detailed as O.C. Enterprise I remained in the
trench. I assumed that position and established my Head Qrs.
at Coy. Hd. Qrs. in front line of trench 113, where it was connected
by telephone with Bn. Hd. Qrs. & where the artillery F.O.O. was in
telephonic communication with his battery.

I have the honour to be
Sir, your obedient servant,
Twenham
Lt-Col. 31st K.W.O.R. Yeo.

Army Form C. 2118.

21/K/2/4

WAR DIARY
or
INTELLIGENCE SUMMARY
(Erase heading not required.)

Vol 4

Confidential

War Diary

21st Bn King's Royal Rifle Corps (Yeoman Rifles)

August 1st to August 31st 1916

Army Form C. 2118.

WAR DIARY or INTELLIGENCE SUMMARY
(Erase heading not required.)

Instructions regarding War Diaries and Intelligence Summaries are contained in F.S. Regs., Part II. and the Staff Manual respectively. Title Pages will be prepared in manuscript.

Place	Date	Hour	Summary of Events and Information	Remarks and references to Appendices
PLOEGSTEERT WOOD	Aug. 1/2	2ᵃᵐ	The Battⁿ held T.112/120 & HUNTERS AV.	F
		3ᵃᵐ	The Battⁿ was relieved by the 15ᵗʰ Bⁿ HANTS, 12ᵗʰ Brigade, at 5 A.m — relief complete by 7.5 A.m. Battⁿ marched by Coys to Billets at PAPOT.	F
PAPOT	2ⁿᵈ/8		Remained in Billets at PAPOT, finding working parties for the R.E., T.103/127.	F
PLOEGSTEERT WOOD		9ᵃ	Relieved 15ᵗʰ Battⁿ HANTS, T. 112/120 & HUNTERS AV., commencing 5 P.m relief completed 6.30 A.m. C. Coy. took over T. 112/113, A.Coy T.114/117, B.T.118/120 & D. Coy. HUNTERS AV.	F
		11ᵇ	A. Coy took over HUNTERS AV. & D. Coy. took over T. 114/117.	F
		9ᵇ	Lt. Col. the Earl of Feversham proceeded to England on Leave to urgent Private Affairs, & Major the Hon. S. Pollards commenced the Battⁿ	F
		11ᵇ	Arrangements were made to discharge 9 smoke along whole of 12 & 3 Inf. Bⁿ front (T. 103/127) at 10 p.m & p.m the 4.1ᵈ Divs. Art Mery to treat enemy's front & support lines with Shrapnel. Wind was unfavourable & operation did not take place.	F
	9/16		Officers took out patrols nightly to enemy's wire & parapet, but failed to encounter any of the enemy so were unable to bring in a prisoner.	F

Army Form C. 2118.

WAR DIARY
or
INTELLIGENCE SUMMARY
(Erase heading not required.)

Instructions regarding War Diaries and Intelligence Summaries are contained in F. S. Regs., Part II. and the Staff Manual respectively. Title Pages will be prepared in manuscript.

Place	Date 1916	Hour	Summary of Events and Information	Remarks and references to Appendices
Ploegsteert Wood	Aug.	15"	The C.O. & Asst Adjt, 11th Battn SHERWOOD FORRESTERS, 70th Infantry Brigade, visited Battn Hqrs to discuss relief on 17th idem. Eight (8) Scouts from same Battn visited & remained with us.	
		16"	Company Commanders, 11th SHERWOOD FORRESTERS, visited their offensive numbers in the trenches, & remained the night.	
		17"	Relieved by 11th Battn SHERWOOD FORRESTERS. Relief complete 7.45 am. Defence schemes, Log Books, & all other documents, including maps, likely to be of value to relieving unit, handed over. Issued wooden Cemetery containers. Trench Tramway Gauges supplied by 69th Infantry Brigade were returned to 69th Infantry Brigade. Surplus baggage & kits belonging to Officers, NCOs & men sent to Moyasse to STEENWERCK (B.17.c.8.6) (between 13" & 18" inst.	
PAPOT		18"	The Battn moved to PAPOT. 4th Divis. Reserve Area. Battn relieved at PAPOT by 69th Infantry Brigade, & marched to billets in 9th Corps Reserve Area (billets 1 mile South of METEREN).	
METEREN		23"	idem, remained there until remarching & engaging in Company Training.	
BAILLEUL		23"	Battn entrained at BAILLEUL WEST Stn, departing 6.28 pm for PONT REMY	
PONT REMY		24"	Detrained at PONT REMY 12.45 am (night of 23/24) & marched to billets at FRANCIERES. Marching as stated on sheet own page.	
FRANCIERES				

WAR DIARY
or
INTELLIGENCE SUMMARY
(Erase heading not required.)

Army Form C. 2118.

Place	Date 1916	Hour	Summary of Events and Information	Remarks and references to Appendices

BAILEUL W. STN PONT REMY	Aug 23/24		Marching out state of Battn :-
			 Officers O.Ranks Horses Mules 2 wheeled 4 wheeled machine Bicycles
			    31 890 47 18 4 vehicles gun handcarts
			                                 17 5 7	

FRANCIERES	24/31		The Battn arrives at FRANCIERES, engaged in Coy. & Battn training & route marching	

Fursham
LIEUT-COL.
KING'S ROYAL RIFLES,
COMNDING. 21ST BATTN.
(YEOMAN RIFLES)
1-9-16.

Army Form C. 2118.

Vol 5

124/41

WAR DIARY
or
INTELLIGENCE SUMMARY
(Erase heading not required.)

Confidential

War Diary.

2nd Bn King's Royal Rifle Corps.
(German Rifles)

September 1st September 30th 1916.

Army Form C. 2118.

WAR DIARY
or
INTELLIGENCE SUMMARY
(Erase heading not required.)

Instructions regarding War Diaries and Intelligence Summaries are contained in F. S. Regs., Part II. and the Staff Manual respectively. Title Pages will be prepared in manuscript.

Place	Date	Hour	Summary of Events and Information	Remarks and references to Appendices
FRANCIÈRES	Sept 1-6		The Battn. remained at Francières engaged in Coy and Batn. training.	
LONGPRÉ	Sep 7		The Battn. entrained at LONGPRÉ - L'EU - CORPS SAINTS - detrained at MÉRICOURT and camped at E.9.a near DERNANCOURT.	
DERNANCOURT	Sep 8		The Battn. rested in camp at DERNANCOURT	
	Sep 9		The Battn. moved into camp at BÉCORDEL (15.7.a)	
	Sep 10		Lt Col the Earl of Feversham and the adjutant and four company commanders visited DEMVILLE wood	
	Sep 11		Battalion rested in camp at BÉCORDEL	
	Sep 12		Battalion moved out of Bécordel POMIÈRES REDOUBT, marching out at 4 p.m.	
	Sep 13		Officers about 7.30 p.m. branched for the night. Officers and men slept out in the bivouacs utilised faced the hamlet + west end of BÉCORT WOOD	
POMIÈRES	Sep 14		Battn. paraded at 6 p.m. to view of Brown Pty Tanks in front of DELVILLE WOOD	

WAR DIARY
INTELLIGENCE SUMMARY

(Erase heading not required.)

Army Form C. 2118.

Place	Date	Hour	Summary of Events and Information	Remarks and references to Appendices
DELVILLE WOOD			The Battalion took part in an attack on the enemy lines in front of DELVILLE WOOD. The 2nd Brigade advanced on our line which passed between the village of PIERS on the left. 8th DECr 1916. The 11th & 21st Battalion were on the left flag the 24th on the right, the 26th & 28th Royal Fusiliers in support. At 17th & 21st Brigade were on the left & the 8th Brigade on the right. The attack started at 6.30 & got into the [illegible] of [illegible] between the SWITCH TRENCH line but noted difficulty particularly on every many [illegible]. The left parties advance parties met with relatively new [illegible] but the second objective the PIERS TRENCH when a few prisoners were taken but the enemy shewed [illegible] to fight. During the ridge of the advance the Battalion suffered rather heavy [illegible] getting to our own lines, however it was found impossible to continue the advance owing to lack of support on the flanks & on the law of the second Objective was consolidated. During the day the Battalion lost 2nd Lieut Henry Gentle & 4 others killed & Capt Walters with 4 others wounded & 2nd Lieut Webb, Gentle & [illegible] were wounded [illegible]. In the evening 15th Bn of Royal Fusiliers arrived forward with Major OXLEY, Major [illegible] and assembled to withdraw to reserve to [illegible]	

Army Form C. 2118.

WAR DIARY
or
INTELLIGENCE SUMMARY
(Erase heading not required.)

Instructions regarding War Diaries and Intelligence Summaries are contained in F. S. Regs., Part II. and the Staff Manual respectively. Title Pages will be prepared in manuscript.

Place	Date	Hour	Summary of Events and Information	Remarks and references to Appendices
			the first forward objective in front of EAUCOURT village. They reached the first objective successfully, costing over the consolidated Druid Trench. "D" Coy 13th Bn of R of E Bn of Leinsters were killed. They were eventually forced back & surrounded & cut off by 50 yards in front of the wood of which was the remnant of Battalion moved into entrenched about 3 G.M. Enfilading machine gun fire, during morning by the right of "D" Coys were that of "D" Coy in retire to Flers to its attack on FLARERS Trench. The attack was supported by Battalion. & in addition to the above killed Capt. Hay & Lieut. Bowles were wounded	
			Killed 4 Officers 5 O.R. Wounded 10 Officers 250 O.R. Missing 70 O.R.	
			1st Battalion passed of the DIARY Dump at 11 a.m. & moved off to the SWITCH TRENCH this Bn remained about an hour & the remainder gone to relieve b FLARE ALLEY also G passed on support of the Battalion moving into the new relieved	

2449 Wt. W14957/M90 750,000 1/16 J.-B.C. & A. Forms/C.2118/12

WAR DIARY
or
INTELLIGENCE SUMMARY

Army Form C. 2118.

Place	Date	Hour	Summary of Events and Information	Remarks and references to Appendices
DERNANCOURT	Sept 14th		The Battalion returned to camp at DERNANCOURT.	
DERNANCOURT	Sept 15		The Battalion rested in camp & the following officers rejoined: Major the Hon G.H. Morgan Lt Shendan 2nd Lt [?] Command of B Coy, Capt Bell. The command of D Coy [?] Lt. Major Thompson. Lt. [?] Capt. Bell wounded & 2nd Lieut. was C.O. his own Capt. B.[?] wounded adj. at [?]. after the [?] meeting.	
	Sept 16-22		The Battalion remained in camp at DERNANCOURT, training for the attack, the construction of [?] trenches etc.	
	Sept 23. 24		Battalion remained in camp at DERNANCOURT.	

[signature] LIEUT.-COL
KING'S ROYAL RIFLES
COMNDING 1/5th BATTN.
(YEOMAN RIFLES.)
1-10-16

Army Form C. 2118.

Vol 6

WAR DIARY
or
INTELLIGENCE SUMMARY

(Erase heading not required.)

Confidential.

War Diary,

21st. Bn., King's Royal Rifle Corps.
(Yeoman Rifles.)

Oct. 1st. to October 31st, 1916.

WAR DIARY or INTELLIGENCE SUMMARY

Army Form C. 2118.

Place	Date	Hour	Summary of Events and Information	Remarks and references to Appendices
DERNANCOURT	2/10/16		The Battalion moved from camp at DERNANCOURT to camp at N.E. of BOTTOMIERS S.2.c.c.	Appendix I
POMMIERS REDOUBT	1/10/16		The battalion remained in camp at DERNANCOURT. N.Z. regiment relieved	O.R.
WOOD LANE	3/10/16		The battalion relieved N.Z. regiment in TEA TRENCH and WOOD LANE	O.R.
WOOD LANE	4/10/16		Battalion remained in WOOD LANE area. In the afternoon the battalion took over FLERS TRENCH from 26th Battn Royal Fusiliers. Four heavy shells dropped all the	O.R.
FLERS TRENCH	5/10/16		evening and night in FLERS TRENCH. Heavy shelling all day especially in the afternoon. 2/Lt Jeaman D.S.O. 1 offr killed ; 4 O.R. ; 1 H.O. wounded O.R. casualties	O.R.
GIRD TRENCH			In the evening the battalion took over the G.1(2) TRENCH from the 28th R.F. Our own heavy artillery kept up a continuous bombardment which was not intense — Enemy replied but not so strong.	Appendix 2

Place	Date	Hour	Summary of Events and Information	Remarks and references to Appendices
EuRD 7/Enam	7/10/16		The morning was normal. Our heavy artillery carried out damage about 12 noon to firing zero short.	Appendix III
		2 p.m.	At 2 p.m. the 28th & 32nd Royal Fusiliers advanced to their objective but were met with very heavy machine gun & rifle fire. D Co. 21st R.R.C. (Capt Shenton) advanced and made a strong point at the map reference junction of the line at N13 c.2.2. B Co then two platoons advanced behind the 32-R.?B but failed to make their strong point owing to their casualties which were very heavy indeed. During the night a communication trench was dug from N19 a-4-5 to N13 c.2.2. and the line was formed up a far as point 74.	
C(R) TRENCH	9/10/16 8/10/16		The disposition were altered in the evening and the Battalion occupied (1R) TRENCH and had (B (2R)) SUPPORT. In the afternoon an infantry party under an R.R.M.C. officer with stretchers helped to evacuate wounded.	
(1R) SUPPORT			Battn HQ moved to FACTORY CORNER.	
	9/10/16 10/10/16		Battalion remained in the line and was relieved on the night 10/10/16-11/10/16 by the Bathalim and	

WAR DIARY or INTELLIGENCE SUMMARY

Army Form C. 2118.

Place	Date	Hour	Summary of Events and Information	Remarks and references to Appendices
FRICOURT	11/10/16		relieved by the 17th Manchester Regt. and 2nd Bn Royal Scots. Battalion entrained at FRICOURT SIDING and	
BECORDEL	12/10/16		proceeded to camp above BECORDEL. Battalion remained in camp.	
BUIRE	13/10/16		Battalion moved into billets at BUIRE.	
BUIRE	14/10/16		Battalion remained in billets at BUIRE.	
AIRAINES	15/10/16		Battalion proceeded by train from EDGE HILL siding to AIRAINES	Appendix IV.
ALLERY	17/10/16		Battalion detrained at AIRAINES and marched to billets at ALLERY.	
	18/10/16		The battalion remained in billets at ALLERY and the day was spent in reorganizing companies and specialists.	
	19/10/16		Battalion marched to LONGPRÉ-LES-CORPS SAINTS station and entrained at 8.57 a.m. (20/10/16)	
METEREN	20/10/16		The battalion detrained at CAESTRE and marched from near METEREN.	
VICTORIA CAMP	20/10/16		The battalion marched from METEREN to VICTORIA CAMP M.3.c.5.5.	Appendix V.

Army Form C. 2118/12.

Army Form C. 2118.

WAR DIARY
or
INTELLIGENCE SUMMARY
(Erase heading not required.)

21st Bn KRRC

Place	Date	Hour	Summary of Events and Information	Remarks and references to Appendices
TRENCHES IN BOIS CARRÉ AREA.	22/10/16		The Battalion relieved the 45th Bn 12th Australian Infantry Brigade in the left sector of the Brigade front. C & D companies in the front line – C on the right and D on the left – B Coy in reserve in BOIS CARRÉ. A Coy remained at VICTORIA CAMP.	Appendix VI.
	23/10/16		Battalion remained in the line – Little hostile activity.	
	24/10/16		Officers sent out patrols nightly – Enemy's wire very strong.	
	28/10/16		On two occasions on in very bad state of repair. Staghound all along the front. Wire fairly good. On the morning of the 26th the Battalion was relieved by the 28th Bn R.F. The enemy shelled fitzcleve & the Brasserie and B.Coy HQrs during the relief & one gun direct hit at LA CLYTTE strafing	Appendix VII
LA CLYTTE	29/10/16		The Battalion remained at LA CLYTTE training and providing working parties for the front line.	31st S&EB

J. W. Hampson
LIEUT.-COL.
COMDNG. 21st BATTN.
KING'S ROYAL RIFLES,
(YEOMAN RIFLES.)

Nominal Roll

2nd Lieut R.W.R Law.

12003	C.S.M.	McEwen	"A"	12870 Rfn. Prest	"D"
R5791	Sergt	Campbell	"A" 16653	Moore	"D"
R19490	Sgt	Robinson	"B" 12905	Hardwick	"D"
12999	Cpl	Chapman	"A" 12313	Walker T.	"D"
12592	Rfn	Faller	"C" 1303o	Matthewson	"D"
12411	-	Taylor	"A" 19165	Ryan E	"D"
12581	-	Rawson	"A" 19074	Rooman W.	"D"
12360	-	Emmerson	"A" 19737	Jowell A.	"D"
12354	-	Cox T.	"A"		
R19400	-	James H.C.	"A"		
12849	-	Gatenby P.	"A"		
12395	-	Robson C.M.	"C"		
12394	-	Liddell T.	"C"		
7607	Cpl	Coe	"B"		
12255	Rfn	Ainsworth	"B"		
12304	"	Coon Jn.	"B"		
12847	-	Kennington	"C"		
13078	-	Holt	"D"		
12506	-	Broadbent	"B"		
12165	-	Peel Jn.	"B"		
12564	-	Woodley	"C"		
12961	-	Mason R.	"C"		
12950	-	Cussey G.J.	"C"		
12127	Sgt	Baker	"D"		
11128	L/Cpl	Manson A.J.	"C"		

Vol. 8.
21st Bn. KRRC.

2-12-16

– to –

31-12-16.

Army Form C. 2118.

WAR DIARY
or
INTELLIGENCE SUMMARY

(Erase heading not required.)

Vol 8

Confidential

War Diary

21st. Bn. King's Royal Rifle Corps.
(Yeoman Rifles)

Dec 1st. to Dec 31st. 1916

ORDERLY ROOM
Date 1 JAN 1917
No.
21st K.R.R. (YEOMAN RIFLES)

WAR DIARY
or
INTELLIGENCE SUMMARY
(Erase heading not required.)

Army Form C. 2118.

Instructions regarding War Diaries and Intelligence Summaries are contained in F. S. Regs., Part II. and the Staff Manual respectively. Title Pages will be prepared in manuscript.

Place	Date	Hour	Summary of Events and Information	Remarks and references to Appendices
Ridgewood	2/12/16 to 7/12/16		The Battalion remained in support providing working parties for the front line.	S.M.
	3/12/16		The 32nd Bn Royal Fusiliers carried out a successful raid on the enemy trenches in the Hollandschour Salient at 12.35 a.m. No retaliation was made by the enemy on our positions in Ridge Wood.	S.M.
"	7/12/16		The Batt. relieved the 26th Batt. R.F. in the left subsector of the line	S.M.
The Line	8/12/16 to 13/12/16		Enemy trench mortar activity greatly increased during this period, most damage being done to the head of Chicory Lane O.T. and the Front Line V.10 to 50 yards on either side of this point. (O.9.a.3.2)	S.M.
	13/12/16		The Battalion was relieved by the 26th Batt R.F. and went back to La Clytte. During the relief of the right front line Company the enemy commenced to bombard Chicory Lane and the Front line up to the Front Line, causing three casualties to our Coy and some damage to trench mortars and blocking Chicory Lane.	S.M.
La Clytte	13/12/16 to 20/12/16 to 14/12/16		The Battalion remained at La Clytte, training and providing working parties for the front line.	S.M.
			At 9 p.m. after a heavy trench mortar bombardment the enemy attempted to raid our trenches near Chicory Lane. Only two of the enemy reached our trench of whom one escaped. The trenches around this point	S.M.

WAR DIARY
or
INTELLIGENCE SUMMARY
(Erase heading not required.)

Army Form C. 2118.

Place	Date	Hour	Summary of Events and Information	Remarks and references to Appendices
Ridgewood	2/2/16 1/7/16 to 3/7/16		On. Battalion remained in support providing working parties for the front line. The 3rd Bn Royal Fusiliers carried out a successful raid on the enemy trenches in the Hollandschen Salient at 12.35 a.m. No retaliation by the enemy on own positions in Ridge Wood	(A) (A)
Ridge Line	7/7/16 8/7/16 9/7/16		Bn. took over the 26th Batt R.F. in the left subsector of the line. The Bn. where the 26th Batt R.F. in the left subsector of the line. Enemy trench mortar activity greatly increased during this period, most activity being to the head of Cheney Lane CT and the road from V to 50 yards	(A) (A)
	10/10/16		to 2 Bn point (C7a 8.2)	(A)
	11/7/16 12/7/16		The Battalion was relieved by the 25th Batt R.F. and moved back to B in the Siding. The step off the right front line Company the Bn commenced to bombard Cheney Lane and the front line trenches causing three casualties a one CPL and some casualties (?)	(A)
			13 ball during Cheney Lane	
No. 4 HH	13/7/16 to 21/7/16 14/7/16		Bn. returned to Camp at Ranifette, training and preparing working parties for the front line. On afternoon of 14th after a heavy trench mortar bombardment the enemy attempted to raid our trenches near Cheney Lane. Only two of the enemy are known to have escaped. The trenches seemed thus found	(A) (A)

2449 Wt. W14957/M90 750,000 1/16 J.B.C. & A. Forms/C.2118/12.

WAR DIARY
or
INTELLIGENCE SUMMARY
(Erase heading not required.)

Instructions regarding War Diaries and Intelligence Summaries are contained in F.S. Regs., Part II. and the Staff Manual respectively. Title Pages will be prepared in manuscript.

Place	Date	Hour	Summary of Events and Information
La Clytte	14/12/16		(O9a H.I.) were rather badly damaged as was The alarm was given at 9.15pm and the La Clytte – Reninghelst road, But no a
"	17/12/16		The Batt. celebrated Christmas on this and cigarettes being provided for the
"	18/12/16		The G.O.C. (General Lawson) inspected
"	20/12/16		The Battalion relieved the 26th Batt. R.F. line trenches in the right (oys) sector and the wire in front of Tuns was also
"	20/12/16 to 24/12/16		The Battalion remained in the line the front line and on the wire in front round the supporting points behind
"	25/12/16		The Batt. was in the line for Christmas bombardment by the Divisional Artillery and slight retaliation. No unusual activity enemy. Though rockets of various colours his line at 5.30pm. Patrols went out every night, encount

WAR DIARY
or
INTELLIGENCE SUMMARY
(Erase heading not required.)

Army Form C. 2118.

Place	Date	Hour	Summary of Events and Information	Remarks and references to Appendices
La Clytte	18/3/16		On a still day rather badly damaged as were the wire in front. Gas alarm was given at 9.15 p.m. and the Battalion turned up on the La Clytte – Reninghelst road, but no instance was required.	R.
"	19/3/16		The Platt estimates plus final on this date. Plum pudding, beer and cigarettes being provided for the men.	R.
"	19/3/16		The G.O.C. (General Capper) inspects the Battalion in training.	R.
"	20/3/16		The Battalion relieves the 26th Batt. R.B. in the front line in front of Ypres. Trenches on the right (A9) were in a fair state of repair but the work in front of them was also weak.	R.
"	21/3/16 to 25/3/16		The Battalion remained in the line, with working parties in the front line and in the support line behind. The Batt. was in the line on Christmas Day in addition, being bombarded by the Divisional Artillery and Trench Batteries present. No unusual activity was shown by the enemy, though bursts of various calibre were sent up from time to time at 8.30 p.m. nights, endangering our British parties.	R.

Army Form C. 2118.

WAR DIARY
or
INTELLIGENCE SUMMARY
(Erase heading not required.)

Instructions regarding War Diaries and Intelligence Summaries are contained in F. S. Regs., Part II and the Staff Manual respectively. Title Pages will be prepared in manuscript.

Place	Date	Hour	Summary of Events and Information	Remarks and references to Appendices
Ridge Wood	27/4/16		The Battalion relieved by the 26th Bn K.R.R. and withdrew to Ridge Wood, where it provided working parties for the front line.	A.
	28/4/16		During the last time the Batt was in this area the enemy have commenced to shell the east and north edges of the wood occasionally with H.E. & Shrapnel. One casualty was suffered by the 25th on the right of the 31st a few more shells were dropped in the wood, but no damage or casualties resulted.	A. A.

J. Wyer. Lieut-Col.
KING'S ROYAL RIFLES,
COMMANDING 21ST BATT'N.
(YEOMAN RIFLES.)

WAR DIARY
or
INTELLIGENCE SUMMARY

Army Form C. 2118.

Place	Date	Hour	Summary of Events and Information	Remarks and references to Appendices
Ridge Wood	2/1/16		The Batt was relieved by the 26th Batt R.F. and withdrew to Ridge Wood, where it provided working parties for the front line. Since the last time the Batt was in this area the enemy had commenced to shell the east and north edges of the wood	JR.
	3/1/16		Occasionally with 4.2" shrapnel. One casualty was suffered	JR.
			On the night of the 3rd a few more shells were dropped in the wood, but no damage or casualties resulted.	JR.

Lieut-Col.
King's Royal Rifles
Commanding. 21st Battn.
(Yeoman Rifles.)

21st BATTALION, THE KING'S ROYAL RIFLE CORPS.
(YEOMAN RIFLES)

1916 Appendix.

December — RIDGEWOOD.

1st — No casualties were suffered by the Batt. during this period in the line. The Batt. was relieved by the 26th Batt. R.F. two days before the usual date in order that an enterprise against the enemy trenches might be arranged by the battalion on our right.

2nd to 7th — The Battalion remained in support providing working parties for the front line.

3rd — The 32nd Bn. Royal Fusiliers carried out a successful raid on the enemy trenches in the Hollandschesur Salient at 12.35am. No retaliation was made by the enemy on our positions in Ridge Wood.

7th — The Batt relieved the 26th Batt. R.F. in the left subsector of the line.

THE LINE.

8th to 13th — Enemy trench mortar activity greatly increased during this period, most damage being done to the head of Chicory Lane C.T. and the front line V for 50 yards on either side of this point (O.7.a.3.2.)

13th — The Battalion was relieved by the 26th Bn. R.F. and went back to LA CLYTTE. During the relief of the right front line Company the enemy commenced to bombard Chicory Lane and the front line with trench mortars causing three casualties to our Coy. and some damage to the front line and blocking Chicory Lane.

LA CLYTTE.

13th to 20th — The Battalion remained at La Clytte training and providing working parties for the front line.

14th — At 9 p.m. after a heavy trench mortar bombardment the enemy attempted to raid our trenches near Chicory Lane. Only two of the enemy reached our trench of whom one escaped. The trenches around this point (O 7 a 4.1.) were rather badly damaged, as was the wire in front. The alarm was given at 9.15pm. and the Battalion formed up on the La Clytte- Reninghelst road, but no assistance was required.

1916 Appendix.

December

17th The Battalion celebrated Christmas on this date, Plum pudding, beer and cigarettes being provided for the men.

19th The G.O.C. (General Lawford) inspected the Battalion in training.

20th The Battalion relieved the 26th Batt. R.F. in the line. Our front line trenches in the right Coys sector were in a bad state of repair and the wire in front of them was also weak.

20th to 27th The Battalion remained in the line, much work being done in the front line and on the wire in front of the right Coy. and round the supporting points behind.

25th The Batt was in the line for Christmas Day. A half-hour's bombardment by the Divisional Artillery and T.M. Batteries provoked slight retaliation. No unusual activity was shown by the enemy, though rockets of various colours were sent up from behind his line at 5.30 p.m. Patrols were sent out every night, encountering no hostile parties.

RIDGE WOOD.

27th The Batt was relieved by the 26th Batt R.F. and withdrew to Ridge Wood, where it provided working parties for the front line. Since the last time the Batt was in this area the enemy have commenced to shell the East and North edges of the wood occasionally with 4.2" shrapnel. One casualty was suffered by on the 29th by this shelling. On the night of the 31st a few more shells were dropped in the wood but no damage or casualties resulted.

G. FOLJAMBE, Lt. Col.
King's Royal Rifles
Commanding 21st Battn (Yeoman Rifles).

21st BATTALION, THE KING'S ROYAL RIFLE CORPS.
(YEOMAN RIFLES)

1916　　　　　　　　　　　　　　　　　　　　　　　Appendix.

December　RIDGEWOOD.

1st　　No casualties were suffered by the Batt. during this period in the line. The Batt. was relieved by the 26th Batt. R.F. two days before the usual date in order that an enterprise against the enemy trenches might be arranged by the battalion on our right.

2nd to 7th　The Battalion remained in support providing working parties for the front line.

3rd　　The 32nd Bn. Royal Fusiliers carried out a successful raid on the enemy trenches in the Hollandschesur Salient at 12.35am. No retaliation was made by the enemy on our positions in Ridge Wood.

7th　　The Batt relieved the 26th Batt. R.F. in the left subsector of the line.

THE LINE.

8th to 13th　Enemy trench mortar activity greatly increased during this period, most damage being done to the head of Chicory Lane C.T. and the front line V for 50 yards on either side of this point (0.7.a.3.2.)

13th　　The Battalion was relieved by the 26th Bn. R.F. and went back to LA CLYTTE. During the relief of the right front line Company the enemy commenced to bombard Chicory Lane and the front line with trench mortars causing three casualties to our Coy. and some damage to the front line and blocking Chicory Lane.

LA CLYTTE.

13th to 20th　The Battalion remained at La Clytte training and providing working parties for the front line.

14th　　At 9 p.m. after a heavy trench mortar bombardment the enemy attempted to raid our trenches near Chicory Lane. Only two of the enemy reached our trench of whom one escaped. The trenches around this point (0 7 a 4.1.) were rather badly damaged, as was the wire in front. The alarm was given at 9.15pm. and the Battalion formed up on the La Clytte- Reninghelst road, but no assistance was required.

21st BATTALION, THE KING'S ROYAL RIFLE CORPS.
(YEOMAN RIFLES)

1916 Appendix.

December — RIDGEWOOD.

1st — No casualties were suffered by the Batt. during this period in the line. The Batt. was relieved by the 26th Batt. R.F. two days before the usual date in order that an enterprise against the enemy trenches might be arranged by the battalion on our right.

2nd to 7th — The Battalion remained in support providing working parties for the front line.

3rd — The 32nd Bn. Royal Fusiliers carried out a successful raid on the enemy trenches in the Hollandschesur Salient at 12.35am. No retaliation was made by the enemy on our positions in Ridge Wood.

7th — The Batt relieved the 26th Batt. R.F. in the left subsector of the line.

THE LINE.

8th to 13th — Enemy trench mortar activity greatly increased during this period, most damage being done to the head of Chicory Lane C.T. and the front line V for 50 yards on either side of this point (O.7.a.3.2.)

13th — The Battalion was relieved by the 26th Bn. R.F. and went back to LA CLYTTE. During the relief of the right front line Company the enemy commenced to bombard Chicory Lane and the front line with trench mortars causing three casualties to our Coy. and some damage to the front line and blocking Chicory Lane.

LA CLYTTE.

13th to 20th — The Battalion remained at La Clytte training and providing working parties for the front line.

14th — At 9 p.m. after a heavy trench mortar bombardment the enemy attempted to raid our trenches near Chicory Lane. Only two of the enemy reached our trench of whom one escaped. The trenches around this point (O 7 a 4.1.) were rather badly damaged, as was the wire in front. The alarm was given at 9.15pm. and the Battalion formed up on the La Clytte- Reninghelst road, but no assistance was required.

1916

Appendix.

December

17th — The Battalion celebrated Christmas on this date, Plum pudding, beer and cigarettes being provided for the men.

19th — The G.O.C. (General Lawford) inspected the Battalion in training.

20th — The Battalion relieved the 26th Batt. R.F. in the line. Our front line trenches in the right Coys sector were in a bad state of repair and the wire in front of them was also weak.

20th to 27th — The Battalion remained in the line, much work being done in the front line and on the wire in front of the right Coy. and round the supporting points behind.

25th — The Batt was in the line for Christmas Day. A half-hour's bombardment by the Divisional Artillery and T.M. Batteries provoked slight retaliation. No unusual activity was shown by the enemy, though rockets of various colours were sent up from behind his line at 5.30 p.m. Patrols were sent out every night, encountering no hostile parties.

RIDGE WOOD.

27th — The Batt was relieved by the 26th Batt R.F. and withdrew to Ridge Wood, where it provided working parties for the front line. Since the last time the Batt was in this area the enemy have commenced to shell the East and North edges of the wood occasionally with 4.2" shrapnel. One casualty was suffered by on the 29th by this shelling. On the night of the 31st a few more shells were dropped in the wood but no damage or casualties resulted.

G. FOLJAMBE, Lt. Col.
King's Royal Rifles
Commanding 21st Battn (Yeoman Rifles).

<u>1916</u>   Appendix.

<u>December</u>

17th   The Battalion celebrated Christmas on this date, Plum pudding, beer and cigarettes being provided for the men.

19th   The G.O.C. (General Lawford) inspected the Battalion in training.

20th   The Battalion relieved the 26th Batt. R.F. in the line. Our front line trenches in the right Coys sector were in a bad state of repair and the wire in front of them was also weak.

20th to 27th   The Battalion remained in the line, much work being done in the front line and on the wire in front of the right Coy. and round the supporting points behind.

25th   The Batt was in the line for Christmas Day. A half-hour's bombardment by the Divisional Artillery and T.M. Batteries provoked slight retaliation. No unusual activity was shown by the enemy, though rockets of various colours were sent up from behind his line at 5.30 p.m. Patrols were sent out every night, encountering no hostile parties.

<u>RIDGE WOOD.</u>

27th   The Batt was relieved by the 26th Batt R.F. and withdrew to Ridge Wood, where it provided working parties for the front line. Since the last time the Batt was in this area the enemy have commenced to shell the East and North edges of the wood occasionally with 4.2" shrapnel. One casualty was suffered by on the 29th by this shelling. On the night of the 31st a few more shells were dropped in the wood but no damage or casualties resulted.

G. FOLJAMBE, Lt. Col.
King's Royal Rifles
Commanding 21st Battn (Yeoman Rifles).

WAR DIARY
// INTELLIGENCE SUMMARY

Vol 9

Confidential

War Diary

21st Bn. King's Royal Rifle Corps.
(Yeoman Rifles).

1st January 1917 to
31st January 1917.

WAR DIARY or INTELLIGENCE SUMMARY

Army Form C. 2118.

(Erase heading not required.)

Place	Date	Hour	Summary of Events and Information	Remarks and references to Appendices
Range Wood	2/9/17	2pm	The Battalion relieved the 26th Batt Royal Fusiliers in the left subsector of the line.	
S.H. Huts	6/9/17		Lieut Colonel the Hon. GN J.S. Roberts, who had commanded the regiment from the 15th September, left us to take up an appointment at Aldershot as Instructor in a school for commanding officers. His departure was regretted by all ranks. Captain Worsley took over temporary command of the regiment.	
"	8/9/17		The Batt was relieved by the 26th Batt Royal Fusiliers and withdrew to Clytte, where it remained, training and providing working parties for the line.	
La Clytte	9/9/17		The Army Commander General Sir Herbert Plumer, inspected the Battalion in training at La Clytte	
"	10/9/17		Captain C.A. Wade, 10th Royal West Kent Regiment, took over command of the regiment.	
"	11/9/17		Lieut G. Tarrant, who has acted as Quartermaster to the Battalion since December 1915, was evacuated sick	
"	14/9/17	11.59pm	The Battalion relieved the 26th Batt Royal Fusiliers in the left subsector of the line	
In the line	20/9/17		2/Lieut J. Breeze Scottish Rifles, attached to this Battalion, was wounded during a trench mortar shoot by the enemy wire	

Army Form C. 2118.

WAR DIARY
or
INTELLIGENCE SUMMARY
(Erase heading not required.)

Place	Date	Hour	Summary of Events and Information	Remarks and references to Appendices
Ridge Wood	20/1/17	11.30pm	The Batt. was relieved by the 26th Batt. Royal Fusiliers, and withdrawing to Ridge Wood, where it remained, providing working parties to the line.	
"	21/1/17	2pm	The heavy frosts have hardened the ground, a football match was played just behind the wood, between the Officers and Sergts of the Battalion, in which, after an exciting game, the Officers won by 1 goal to nil.	
	24/1/17	2pm	The Battalion relieved the 26th Batt. Royal Fusiliers in the left subsector of the line.	
	25/1/17	2.30pm	A bombardment of the enemy's front line system opposite our new corner, by our howitzers and light trench mortars in cooperation with the artillery. Considerable damage was done to the enemy trenches and wire, and the enemy's retaliation was slight. Lieut. Colonel J. Mc E. Jarvis of the 10th Batt. Queens Royal West Surrey Regt assumed command of this Battalion.	
	26/1/17			

Walter Jarvis
Lieut-Col.
KING'S ROYAL RIFLES,
COMMDG. 21st BATTN.
(YEOMAN RIFLES.)

WAR DIARY
INTELLIGENCE SUMMARY

Army Form C. 2118.

of 21st Bn K.R.R.C. Vol 10

Place	Date	Hour	Summary of Events and Information	Remarks and references to Appendices
The Line	1/9/17		The Battalion was relieved by the 26th Batt. R.Rus. and proceeded to rest at La Clytte, where it remained, training and providing working parties to the line.	(sgd)
La Clytte	5/9/17		The Batt. relieved the 26th Batt. Royal Fusiliers in the left subsector of the line. No particular enemy activity was remarked and patrols, which went out every night, reported no enemy in NO MANSLAND.	(sgd)
			The Battalion was relieved by the 26th Batt. R. Fus. and withdrew to Ridgewood, about to remained providing working parties to the line.	(sgd)
Ridgewood	10/9/17		The Battalion relieved the 26th Batt. Royal Fusiliers in the left subsector of the line.	(sgd)
Ridgewood	16/9/17			Map sheet 28 (Wytschaete)
Old Fus	17/9/17		At 4.10 p.m. the enemy commenced a very violent bombardment of our Reserve line and the Redoubts in Bois Carré (N.12.b) At about 4.30 p.m. this spread down Shinny Lane (our right c.t.) to the right sector front line; and the Telephone wire cut immediately afterwards. Owing to the mist, and the heavy bombardment communication with the parts of the line affected was impossible. Soon after dusk a small party of the enemy is believed to have entered our trench O.7.2, and captured the crew of a Lewis Gun, which was in an isolated position in a salient in this trench. Our trenches O.9.1 & O.9.2 were completely blown in - being a series of "minenwerfer" craters, and	

WAR DIARY
or
INTELLIGENCE SUMMARY

Army Form C. 2118.

Place	Date	Hour	Summary of Events and Information	Remarks and references to Appendices
The Line			The remainder of our front line redoubts and reserve line around Poars Carré were severely damaged in places. Our total casualties were 7 Killed, 14 Wounded, 5 Missing. The Battalion in ull had 30 casualties.	J.M.
The Line	16/9/19		We had no officer casualties. The 18th Batt K.R.Rifles came into the line on our right taking the place of the 10th Batt. Queens R.W.S. Regt which proceeded to Steenvoorde. To train for operations against the Hollandscheschuur Salient. The Battalion was relieved by the 26th Batt. R. Brs. and withdrew to Chippawa Camp (Reninghelst), where it rested and carried out training.	J.M.
The Line	22/9/19		Making facilities were less numerous than usual, and more men had more rest and more comfortable quarters.	J.M.
Chippawa Camp	24/9/19		The 10th Batt Queens R.W.S. Regt carried out a most successful raid against the Hollandscheschuur Salient penetrating to the support line, capturing 1 Officer and 54 men & bring a machine gun.	J.M.
"	25/9/19		The Battalion relieved the 26th Batt. R. Brs. in the left subsector of the line.	J.M.

Talbot Farr.

LIEUT-COL.
KING'S ROYAL RIFLES,
COMMDING. 21st BATTN.
(YEOMAN RIFLES)

WAR DIARY or INTELLIGENCE SUMMARY

Army Form C. 2118.

21 KRR Vol XI

Place	Date	Hour	Summary of Events and Information	Remarks and references to Appendices
The Line	1/3/17 to 6/3/17		No particular hostile activity. The tour in the line considerably quieter than the tour in the previous front line to the right of CHICORY LANE. Battalion was relieved by 26th Royal Fusiliers and	Ref W/Diaries Attached Sketch map. See Appendix I
RIDGE WOOD	8/3/17		proceeded to RIDGE WOOD, when it remained for the time in Brigade Reserve providing working parties.	
The Line	12/3/17		Relieved 26th Bn Royal Fusiliers. A very quiet tour in the line.	See Appendix II
LA CLYTTE	16/3/17		Relieved by 26th Bn Royal Fusiliers and proceeded to LA CLYTTE when training was carried out.	See Appendix III
STEENVOORDE	21/3/17 22/3/17 23/3/17		Battalion proceeded to STEENVOORDE area and was billeted in farms in the area. Battalion moved by Lillebek. Training carried on by companies.	Weather bad, not attacks much – See Appendix IV
	24/3/17 25/3/17		Inspection by the Army Commander. Training carried out by companies.	

WAR DIARY
or
INTELLIGENCE SUMMARY

Army Form C. 2118.

Place	Date	Hour	Summary of Events and Information	Remarks and references to Appendices
STEENWOORDE	28/3/17		Company training and practice in the annual by Platoon and by companies -	
	29/3/17		Battalion route marching in fighting order -	
	30/3/17		Battalion practice in the attack.	
	31/3/17		Battalion practice in Brigade competition for the right to hoist 124 M.G. Cy in trench mortar - M.R. 6 guns - 3 - The Battalion lost	

Talbot Janno.
LIEUT.-COL
KING'S ROYAL RIFLES,
COMNDING. 21ST BATTN.
(YEOMAN RIFLES.)

Army Form C. 2118.

WAR DIARY
or
INTELLIGENCE SUMMARY

(Erase heading not required.)

No 12

CONFIDENTIAL —

WAR DIARY

of

21st Bn. King's Royal Rifle Corps
(Yeoman Rifles)

From 1st April to 30th April
1917.

Army Form C. 2118.

WAR DIARY
or
INTELLIGENCE SUMMARY

(Erase heading not required.)

Instructions regarding War Diaries and Intelligence Summaries are contained in F. S. Regs., Part II. and the Staff Manual respectively. Title Pages will be prepared in manuscript.

Place	Date	Hour	Summary of Events and Information	Remarks and references to Appendices
STEENVOORDE	1/4/17		124th Inf. Bde. Sports. — Prizes won by the battalion:— Relay Race for Runners — 1st Prize. 1st Team home in Cross Country Race. Obstacle Race 1st Prize. 7th Brigade Football Tournament won 1 to 12 Bn. Final. 2/1st K.R.R.C. 5 Goals 32nd R.F. 0 goals.	
STEENVOORDE	2/4/17		Battle practised attack in new formation. Taken over trenches. A flag barrage was provided. The new formation is a district success especially in watching over all the ground we were found before the enemy barrage could come down. Weather fine.	
STEENVOORDE	3/4/17		Battle practised. Musketry in a.m.	
STEENVOORDE	4/4/17		Brigade attack practised. — Difficulty in keeping direction experienced. Impetuous to certain work employed and.	See Appendix I.

WAR DIARY or INTELLIGENCE SUMMARY

Army Form C. 2118.

(Erase heading not required.)

Place	Date	Hour	Summary of Events and Information	Remarks and references to Appendices
STEENVOORDE	5/4/17		Brigade attack grain practices. Very successful - B.	
DICKEBUSCH	6/4/17		The Battalion marched to DICKEBUSCH. Two companies accommodated in BATTERSEA (A & D) — Hqrs C. and Reserve & 12th Inf Bde holding ST ELOI sector.	See Appendix IV
			2 OR men and ofphir staff from this Battalion in the line - and went for working parties in the 12th Inf Bde zone.	Appendix III
			The battalion received 122nd Inf Bn in ST ELOI sector. 2nd Lieut J. S. Leople was wounded while crossing Capt. W. J. Watson who was wounded, in the time. B. 122nd Inf Bde returned 12th Inf Bde reporting to battalion. B	
DICKEBUSCH	12/4/17		in reserve in DICKEBUSCH area	Appendix III A
	16/4/17		12th Inf Bde returned 121st Inf Bde Battalion in reserve in DICKEBUSCH area	Appendix III B
	17/4/17 18/4/17			
	23/4/17		Battalion remained in reserve in DICKEBUSCH area. Nothing particular	Appendix III C

Army Form C. 2118.

WAR DIARY
or
INTELLIGENCE SUMMARY
(Erase heading not required.)

Place	Date	Hour	Summary of Events and Information	Remarks and references to Appendices
Yperesen	26/4/17		C o D Coy returned at BATTERSEA (H 32 b 6 9) & Tps on landing E 1/17th London Rgt, 174 Division. Btn. C. D. Coy. remainder at MICMAC CAMP (H 31 a 9 5).	See Appendix IV
	30/4/17		2/Lt T.D. Walsh R.R. was wounded 10/9/16 rejoined the Battalion. Casualties during the month:- Killed Wounded Officers — 1 (2/Lt T.B. Joseph) O.R. — 3 to trench mortar Total Nil 4	

Talbot Jannan
LIEUT.-COL.
KING'S ROYAL RIFLES,
COMMDING. 21st BATTN.
(YEOMAN RIFLES.)

Army Form C. 2118.

WAR DIARY
~~INTELLIGENCE SUMMARY~~
(Erase heading not required.)

Vol 13

Confidential

War Diary

21st Bt. Kings Royal Rifle Corps
(Yeoman Rifles)

1st May to 31st May 1917.

Army Form C. 2118.

WAR DIARY
or
INTELLIGENCE SUMMARY
(Erase heading not required.)

Instructions regarding War Diaries and Intelligence Summaries are contained in F. S. Regs., Part II. and the Staff Manual respectively. Title Pages will be prepared in manuscript.

Place	Date	Hour	Summary of Events and Information	Remarks and references to Appendices
MICMAC & DICKEBUSCH	May 1 and 2		The Bn was in camp at MICMAC and DICKEBUSCH and supplied large working parties for the line day and night. Dispositions H.Q. C & D Coys at MICMAC. A & B Coys at DICKEBUSCH.	
	May 3		The Bn proceeded by march route to ALBERTA Camp being relieved by the 20th Bn D.L.I.	App. I
ALBERTA (RENINGHELST)	May 4 to May 16		The Bn remained at ALBERTA Camp & working parties were supplied by two Coys alternately; the other 2 Coys trained. On May 6. to celebrate the anniversary of the arrival of the Bn in France a Concert and Play were given by the Bn in the Y.M.C.A. Concert Hall in RENINGHELST.	
G.21.A.2.7. Sheet 27.	May 17		The Bn was relieved by the 16th Bn Royal West Kent Regt. and proceeded by march to the G.21 a 2.7. where the Bn bivouacked for the night.	
EPERLECQUES	May 18		The Bn left for GANSPETTE training area. The Bn entrained at POPERINGHE at 7 AM and detrained at WATTEN at 11 AM and marched to billets at EPERLECQUES.	App. II

Army Form C. 2118.

WAR DIARY
or
INTELLIGENCE SUMMARY
(Erase heading not required.)

Place	Date	Hour	Summary of Events and Information	Remarks and references to Appendices
EPERLECQUES	May 19 to May 31		The Bn. trained for offensive operations. The first 6 days of the training were devoted to Coy. & Bn. training. On May 24 an unfortunate accident during Rifle Grenade practice, probably caused by a defective cartridge, resulted in the following casualties. Killed 1 O.R.; wounded 1 Officer (2nd Lt. A. LESLIE) and 8 O.R. The remainder of the time was devoted to Brigade in attack. The training was good and the health of the men was considerably improved by the change.	

Tubb Hanning
LIEUT-COL.
KING'S ROYAL RIFLES,
COMMDNG. 21st BATTN.
(YEOMAN RIFLES.)

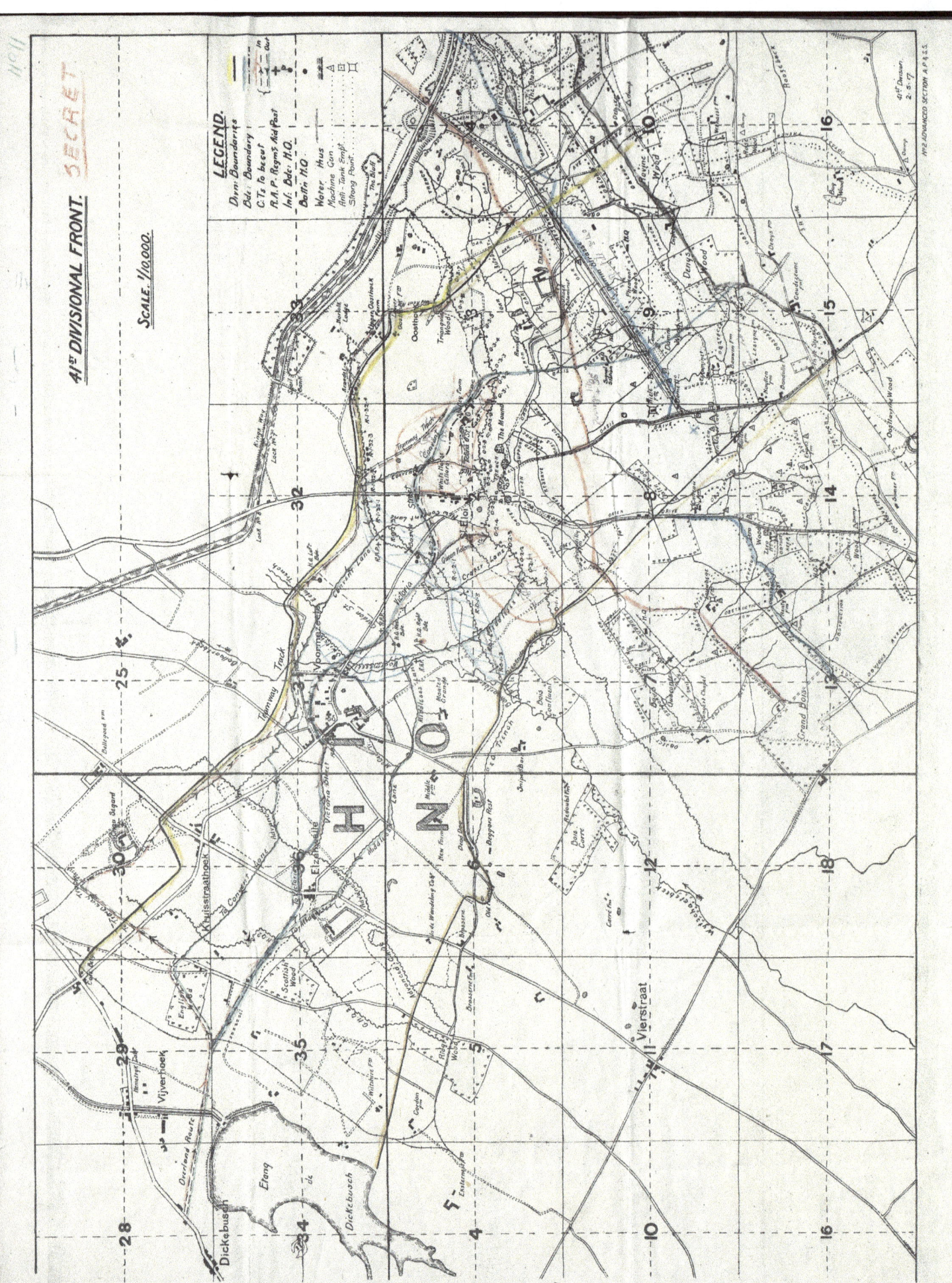

WAR DIARY
or
INTELLIGENCE SUMMARY

Army Form C. 2118.

174/1
Vol 15

Place	Date	Hour	Summary of Events and Information	Remarks and references to Appendices
METEREN	July 16th 1916		The Battalion was in training at METEREN	
"	18th		The Battalion proceeded by march route to CURRAGH CAMP, WESTOUTRE	
WESTOUTRE	19th to 22nd		The Battalion proceeded to ASCOT CAMP, WESTOUTRE where Training was continued	
	23rd to 29th		The Battalion proceeded by march route to RIDGE WOOD and Supplied working parties for the Front Line	
	30th		The Battalion proceeded to take up its position in support to the 123rd Infantry Brigade for an attack on the enemy system of trenches	APPENDIX

Taylor Innes
Lieut Col
Commanding 21st Bn KRRC

WAR DIARY or INTELLIGENCE SUMMARY

21 KRRC Vol 10 August

Army Form C. 2118.

Place	Date	Hour	Summary of Events and Information	Remarks and references to Appendices
R/MAP ZILLEBEKE SHEET 28 NW & SHEET 28 NE 3	30th to 31st JULY		On the night of the 30/31st July 1917 the Battalion took up its position in support to the 123rd. Inf. Bde. for an attack on the enemy system of trenches. The Battalion was at the disposal of the G.O.C. 123rd. Infantry Brigade. Whilst proceeding to the assembly position the Battalion suffered a few casualties by mustard gas shells. At dawn on the 31st July the Artillery barrage opened and the attack by the 123rd Infantry Brigade commenced. The attack took place during heavy rainstorms which made progress extremely difficult. Stiff fighting took place throughout the day and the Battalion moved forward early in the evening. About 7p.m. the enemy counter attacked on the right flank of the 123rd. Brigade. A and D Companies moved forward and met the attack, causing the enemy to withdraw with heavy losses. 2nd Lieut. W.B. HARMON was killed whilst leading his Company to the attack. At dusk A and D Companies returned to their original	APPENDIX I.

Appendix I

Copy No 2

SECRET.

YEOMAN RIFLES, OPERATION ORDER NO. 29.
by
LIEUT-COL. TALBOT McL. JARVIS, D.S.O.
----

1. **INTENTION.**

    (Zero hour will be notified later).

    The 41st Division will attack at a date to be fixed later on a frontage from FORRET FARM on the right to the KLEIN ZILLEBEKE ROAD on the left.
    The 123rd Infantry Brigade plus the 21st Bn. K.R.R.C. and the 26th Bn. Royal Fusiliers will be on the North of the Canal and the 122nd Infantry Brigade on the South of the Canal.
    The 124th Infantry Brigade less these two Battalions will be Divisional Reserve.
    The 21st Bn. K.R.R.C. will be in support of 123rd Infantry Brigade and the 26th Bn. Royal Fusiliers in Reserve.

2. **OBJECTIVES.**

    The red, blue and green lines as shewn on attached map.
    The green line to be eventually the Front Line, the blue line the Support and the red the Reserve Line.
    Should the opportunity offer it may be decided to exploit a success by a further advance on ZANVORDE.
    One Brigade of the 47th Division, will be held in readiness for this on Z day in G.H.Q. 2nd Line.
    Dispositions as shewn on attached map.
    From Z hour the 21st Bn. K.R.R.C. will be ready to move up to any position as may be ordered by the G.O.C. 123rd Infantry Brigade.

3. **BARRAGE.**

    There will be the usual preliminary bombardment barrage and protective barrage according to the time table issued to Company Commanders and as shewn on attached map.

    There will be in addition a Machine Gun barrage in front of each objective from Z hour until Zero plus 70 minutes when it will be ready to answer any S.O.S. call.

4. **MEDICAL.**

    R.A.P. will be established at (1) Junction CATERPILLAR TRACK and IDEAL AVENUE (2) OAK AVENUE O.4.b.2½.9.
    The collecting post for these will be at NORFOLK BRIDGE.

5. **CONTACT AEROPLANES.**

    One contact aeroplane with three broad white bands on the Fuselage and (with black board on the left lower plane) will be up from Zero to Zero plus 3 hours and will call for flares (No. 3 Red) by claxon-horn or by firing a white rocket.
    Flares must be supplemented by waving helmets, maps, papers etc.
    A Wireless plane which will be up all day from Zero plus 1 hour and will warn Infantry by a Green Flare that a counterattack is developing north of the Canal and by a Red Flare if south of the Canal and will also transmit any Infantry Messages calling for barrage.
    Patrols temporarily pushed forward to cover consolidation will not light flares.

6. **R.E. and PIONEERS.**

   On Y/Z night a Pontoon Bridge at O.4.a.77. capable of conveying Infantry in fours will be constructed. The site already is being marked by small notice boards. Infantry must break step when using the bridge.
   There will be no working party on Y day or Y/Z night.

7. **R.E. DUMPS.**

   Divisional at BRASSERIE N.6.a.11.
   Advanced at IMP DUMP O.4.a.8.8.

8. **T.M.B's.**

   One Officer and Gun Team from 124th L.T.M.B. will join the Battalion on X day and will be attached for the operations.

9. **PRISONERS.**

   Prisoners will be escorted to the BRASSERIE at N.6.a.10.10. escort being a proportion of 5% where they will be handed over to the A.P.M. 10th Corps and recei pt taken. They must not be searched forward of this. All documents, trophies etc., will be sent there without delay and escorts must know where and by whom prisoners were taken and see that (1) Officers, N.C.O's and men are kept apart and not allowed to converse on the way down (2) That no documents are destroyed by prisoners on the way down.

10. **IDENTIFICATION.**

    No letters or papers capable of giving information likely to be of value to the enemy must be taken into the attack.

11. **EQUIPMENT.**

    Equipment as laid down in S.S.135 and for the last offensive.

12. **CODE.**

    The Code Signal for communicating with Aeroplanes will be used whenever possible. These have already been issued to O.C. Companies.

13. **RATIONS.**

    On moving into assembly positions on Y/Z night rations for Z day will be carried on the men. Rations for Z plus 1 day will be drawn on Z evening from IMP DUMP at O.4.a.8.8.

14. **DUMPS - WATER.**

    Water at NORFOLK LODGE BRIDGE I.33.d.3.6.
    At Norfolk Bridge there will be a reserve dump of Petrol tins. All Petrol tins available will be salvaged and taken to the nearest water point.
    Allotment of water will be on the scale of a 1/3rd of a gallon per man per day.

15. **DUMPS - AMMUNITION.**

    Left Brigade Dump will be at I.34.c.5.0.

16. **KIT.**

    As laid down in S.S. 135 and the last offensive.

17. **SIGNAL COMMUNICATION.**

    The arrangement with Brigade Forward Party will be the same as on the 7th June.

18. **DETAILS.**

    Details of the 124th Infantry Brigade will remain at DEZOW CAMP under charge of Major A.T. Watson.

    All the necessary details of the scheme has already been explained to the Officers concerned.

    No orders or maps will be taken forward of Brigade Headquarters.

    Embodied copy a/ds/ for OC 21 KRRC

26/7/17.

Copy nº 1	File	Copy nº 9	B Coy
2	War Diary	10	C
3	123rd Inf Bde	11	D
4	124 "	12	Transport Officer
5	C.O.	13	Quarter Master
6	2nd in Command	14	Medical Officer
7	Adjutant		
8	A Coy		

WAR DIARY or INTELLIGENCE SUMMARY

Army Form C. 2118.

Place	Date	Hour	Summary of Events and Information	Remarks and references to Appendices
	1st Aug 1917		Position in the vicinity of BATTLE WOOD. On the morning of the 1st. August a further attack was made by the 123rd. Infantry Brigade, the Battalion being in close support between the points I.36.a.3.3. and the KLEIN ZILLEBEKE ROAD. The weather conditions were extremely severe and great difficulties were experienced through the heavy condition of the ground. On the evening of the 1st. August the Battalion relieved the 20th Bn. Durham Light Infantry in the left Battalion Sector, with Headquarters at the CATERPILLAR at I.31.a.9.8½. There were a few casualties during the Relief including 2nd Lieut. H.T. WATTS who was severely wounded. There were no trenches in the Front Line and the climatic conditions rendered their construction impossible. Many wounded were	APPENDIX II. APPENDIX III

WAR DIARY
or
INTELLIGENCE SUMMARY

Army Form C. 2118.

Place	Date	Hour	Summary of Events and Information	Remarks and references to Appendices
	2nd to 6th Aug.		found in the vicinity of the Front Line and Stretcher Bearers worked continuously throughout the night carrying them over almost impassable ground.	A
			The Battalion Consolidated the position won, strong points were erected and garrisoned. On the night of the 3/4th August the Battalion was relieved in the Front Line by the 32nd Br. Royal Fusiliers and took up a position in the old German First Line.	A
	6th Aug.		The Battalion was relieved by the 10th Bn. Queens R.W.S. Regt. (123rd Infantry Brigade) on the night of the 6/7th August and proceeded to Camp in SCOTTISH WOOD H.36.c.50.25, and remained in Reserve to the 123rd Infantry Brigade.	APPENDIX IV
	7th		The Battalion was re-organised and refitted. Battle was	A

Army Form C. 2118.

WAR DIARY
or
INTELLIGENCE SUMMARY
(Erase heading not required.)

Place	Date	Hour	Summary of Events and Information	Remarks and references to Appendices
SCOTTISH WOOD	8th Aug.		Proceeded at ELZENWALLE. The Battalion was inspected by the Divisional Commander who expressed his appreciation of the good work of the Battalion during the preceding operation.	
H 35.c. CENTRAL	9th Aug.		The Battalion moved Camp to WILTSHIRE FARM H 35.c. Central immediately after the Divisional Commander's inspection. The reorganisation and completion of equipment and necessaries were carried out.	A.A. A.A.
	10th Aug.		The Battalion proceeded from WILTSHIRE FARM to relieve the 10th Bn. Royal West Kent Regiment in the front line of the left Divisional Sector. A and D Coys in the Front Line, B and C Coys in close support.	APPENDIX V A.A.

Army Form C. 2118.

WAR DIARY
or
INTELLIGENCE SUMMARY

(Erase heading not required.)

Instructions regarding War Diaries and Intelligence Summaries are contained in F. S. Regs., Part II. and the Staff Manual respectively. Title Pages will be prepared in manuscript.

Place	Date	Hour	Summary of Events and Information	Remarks and references to Appendices
	11th to 14th Aug.		The Battalion continued the consolidation of the line, strong points were erected in advance of the Front Line and working parties from the Support Battalion (32nd Bn. Royal Fusiliers) assisted in the construction of new defences.	
	14th.		On the morning of the 14th. August a raid was attempted against enemy dugouts. The heavy condition of the ground and heavy enemy machine gun fire prevented the party from reaching their objectives and they returned with slight casualties.	APPENDIX VI /SK.
	14th 15th		On the night of the 14th/15th. August the Battalion was relieved by the 16th. Bn. Sherwood Foresters and proceeded to camp at WILTSHIRE FARM, H.35.c. Central. The enemy made a counter	APPENDIX VII /SK

Army Form C. 2118.

WAR DIARY
or
INTELLIGENCE SUMMARY

(Erase heading not required.)

Place	Date	Hour	Summary of Events and Information	Remarks and references to Appendices
THIESHOUCK	15th.		attack on the morning of the 15th. August and was successfully repulsed by "D" Company and the relieving Company of the Sherwood Foresters. On the evening of the 15th. the Battalion was conveyed by motor busses to THIESHOUCK Q.35.6.5.4. Sheet 27.S.E.	APPENDIX VIII 6A 6A
do.	16th.		Reorganisation and refitting were carried out.	6A
do.	17th.		The Brigade was inspected by the Corps Commander.	6A
do.	18th.		The Brigade was inspected by the Army Commander who expressed his appreciation of the work of the Brigade during the recent operations. On the night of the 18th. August the enemy dropped bombs in the	

Copy to
APPENDIX X

Operation Order No 5
by
Lieut Col Talbot McL Ponsonby D.S.O.
Commanding 21st Bn the Kings Royal Rifle Corps
Saturday 25th August 1917.

1. The Battalion will continue the march to TATINGHAM tomorrow. Distance about 11 miles.
2. Order of march HQ Coy B.C Bugle Band, Band D.A 1st Line Transport
3. The Battalion will parade at 7.30am in Column of Route on main LE NIEPPE – ARQUES Road. Head of column at Crossroads T.11.a. facing south west.
4. The same distances, march discipline etc as for today
5. Reveille 5am Breakfast 6am. Dinner 12.30pm
6. Sick Parade 6.30am at B Coy Billet. The Sick will rejoin their Coy on Battalion parade
7. Baggage will be stacked at the various Headquarters by 6.30am. The Transport Officer will arrange to collect from the various dumps.
8. When marching at ease, rifles will invariably be slung over either shoulder.
9. OC Coys will send a report to Bn HQ on arrival at the new billets, stating the time their Coy arrived in billets and any casualties which may have occurred on the line of march.

2

10. Capt G.J.L BURTON will perform the duties of 2nd in Command on the march to morrow. He will ensure that the Battalion billets are left scrupulously clean, and that all latrines are filled in.

C.A.Brown. Major
25.8.17   O/C 6th K.R.R.C.

Issued as 3 copies to known.
   Copy No 1 A Coy
     "   " 2 B Coy
     "   " 3 C Coy
     "   " 4 D Coy
     "   " 5 Lew Deroy
     "   " 6 Transport Officer
     "   " 7 R.S.M
     "   " 8 File

WAR DIARY
or
INTELLIGENCE SUMMARY

(Erase heading not required.)

Army Form C. 2118.

Place	Date	Hour	Summary of Events and Information	Remarks and references to Appendices
THIENNES	19th to 24th		vicinity of the Brigade, causing heavy casualties to the 10th Bn. Queen's R.W.S. Regt. No casualties were caused in the Battalion. Training was carried out under Battalion arrangements.	N/A
	25th		The Battalion proceeded by march route to the Renascure Area and was accommodated for the night in the vicinity of LE NIEPPE.	APPENDIX IX
LE NIEPPE	26th		The Battalion proceeded by march route to the Army Training Area and arrived at its destination, TATINGHEM, about noon. All Companies were settled in billets at 2.30 p.m.	APPENDIX X
TATINGHEM	27th to 30th		Training was carried out under Battalion arrangements in the Army Training Area.	N/A

WAR DIARY
or
INTELLIGENCE SUMMARY

Place	Date	Hour	Summary of Events and Information	Remarks and references to Appendices
TATINGHEM	31st Aug.		The Brigade was inspected by the Field Marshal, Commanding-in-Chief, British Armies in France.	1st.
			Casualties during the month	
			KILLED 3 OFFICERS 26 O.R.	
			WOUNDED 10 OFFICERS 253 O.R.	
			MISSING — 9 O.R.	
			Officers killed	
			Major ARTHUR TOWARD WATSON	
			Capt. CHARLES OWEN SPENCER SMITH	
			2nd Lieut. WILFRED BALDWIN HARMON	

Talbot Ponsonby
LIEUT.-COL.
KING'S ROYAL RIFLES,
COMMANDING, 21ST BATTN.
(YEOMAN RIFLES)

21st. Bn. King's Royal Rifle Corps
(Yeoman Rifles)

War Diary 1st Sept 1917 to 30th Sept 1917

Army Form C. 2118.

WAR DIARY
or
INTELLIGENCE SUMMARY
(Erase heading not required.)

Instructions regarding War Diaries and Intelligence Summaries are contained in F. S. Regs., Part II. and the Staff Manual respectively. Title Pages will be prepared in manuscript.

Place	Date	Hour	Summary of Events and Information	Remarks and references to Appendices
TATINGHEM	1st.		The Battalion carried out training as the 2nd Army Training Area. Under Battalion arrangements. Specialist Classes of Signallers, Lewis Gunners, Snipers, Scouts and Sketch Beavers were organised	
	2nd		The Divisional Commander presented Medal Ribbons to Officers and men who has received Awards during recent operations.	
	3rd to 7th.		Training was carried out and Musketry Practice was fired at the Ranges in the Training Area.	
	8th		A Brigade Practice Attack was carried out over Practice ground.	APPENDIX. 1
	9th.		A Brigade Church Service was held at LONGUENESS.	
	10th		A Brigade Practice Attack was carried out over the same ground as on the 8th Sept.	APPENDIX II

Army Form C. 2118.

WAR DIARY
or
INTELLIGENCE SUMMARY
(Erase heading not required.)

Instructions regarding War Diaries and Intelligence Summaries are contained in F. S. Regs., Part II. and the Staff Manual respectively. Title Pages will be prepared in manuscript.

Place	Date	Hour	Summary of Events and Information	Remarks and references to Appendices
TATINGHEM	Sept. 11th.		The Battalion attended a Gas Demonstration and Lecture by the Divisional Gas Officer.	
do.	12th.		A Brigade Practice attack was held over the same ground as on the 10th.	
do.	13th.		Training was carried out under Company Arrangements.	
	14th.		The Battalion proceeded by march route to the WALLON CAPPEL AREA and was accommodated in billets near OXELAERE.	APPENDIX III
OXELAERE	15th.		The Battalion entrained the march to the Forward Area and proceeded to THIESHOOK. Tent accommodation was provided.	APPENDIX IV
	16th.		The Battalion proceeded by march route to RIDGE WOOD.	APPENDIX V
RIDGE WOOD	17th.		The Battalion was completely fitted out with S.A.A. Grenades &c.	

WAR DIARY
or
INTELLIGENCE SUMMARY
(Erase heading not required.)

Army Form C. 2118.

Place	Date	Hour	Summary of Events and Information	Remarks and references to Appendices
SHREWSBURY FOREST	19th to 22nd	5.15 p.m.	the equipment required for the forthcoming Operations. B and C Companies marched from the Camp at RIDGE WOOD to relieve the 11th Bn. Hants. Regt. in the line.	APPENDIX VI
		7h a.	A and D Companies proceeded to their Preliminary assembly position in VOORMEZEELE.	APPENDIX VII
	18th	10.30 p.m.	A and D Companies moved forward to the Battalion Battle Reserve and took disposed in depth between the Battalion Boundaries from the Front Line to CANADA STREET TRENCH (inclusive). See Appendix VIII	
	23rd		The Battalion entrained from OUDEROOM and was conveyed to CAËSTRE	APPENDIX IX

WAR DIARY
or
INTELLIGENCE SUMMARY

(Erase heading not required.)

Army Form C. 2118.

Place	Date	Hour	Summary of Events and Information	Remarks and references to Appendices
LE PEUPLIER	26th to 27th		Arriving in billets at LE PEUPLIER at 11 p.m.	
	28th		Training was carried out under Battalion arrangements.	APPENDIX I
			The Battalion was conveyed by motor buses to the GHYVELDE AREA and encamped near the village of GHYVELDE.	
	29th		The Battalion was inspected by the Divisional Commander who expressed his appreciation of the work of the Battalion during the recent operations.	
	30th		Training was carried out under Battalion arrangements.	

L.W.Brown. Major
KING'S ROYAL RIFLES
COMMANDING 11th BN.
11th BN. KING'S ROYAL RIFLES

124 I.B.
G.74.

TO:- Officer Commanding,
10th Bn. "Queens" R.W.S.Regt.
26th Bn. Royal Fusiliers.
32nd Bn. Royal Fusiliers.
21st Bn. K.R.R.C.

  During all moves in XVth Corps area, minimum distances between Units will be maintained as follows :-

  Between Infantry Companies - 200 yards.
    " Other Units and
  Sections of Transport of
  equivalent road space - 200 yards.

Captain,
Brigade Major,
124th. Infantry Brigade.

30/9/17.

WAR DIARY
or
INTELLIGENCE SUMMARY

21st Battalion King's Royal Rifle Corps.
(Yeoman Rifles)

War Diary 1st Oct. 1917 to 31st Oct. 1917.

Army Form C. 2118.

WAR DIARY
or
INTELLIGENCE SUMMARY
(Erase heading not required.)

Instructions regarding War Diaries and Intelligence Summaries are contained in F.S. Regs., Part II. and the Staff Manual respectively. Title Pages will be prepared in manuscript.

Place	Date	Hour	Summary of Events and Information	Remarks and references to Appendices
GHYVELDE	1st to 5th		The Battalion carried out training on the beach near BRAYDUNES.	
LA PANNE	6th		The Battalion relieved the 1/10th MANCHESTER REGT. in the Coast Defence Sector W.9.d.9.9 on the EAST, to the Franco-Belgian Frontier on the West V.23.d.3.5. A and C Coys were in the line, B and D Coys in close support.	APPENDIX I
	7th to 14th		B and D Coys carried out training; and provided working parties at COXYDE BAINS.	
OOST DUNKERQUE BAINS	15th		The Battalion was relieved in the Coast Defence Sector by the 18th Bn. K.R.R.C. and proceeded to MIDDLESEX CAMP which was taken over from the 2nd. Battalion Durham Light Infantry.	APPENDIX II

2449 Wt. W14957/M90 750,000 1/16 J.B.C. & A. Forms/C.2118/12.

WAR DIARY
or
INTELLIGENCE SUMMARY

(Erase heading not required.)

Army Form C. 2118.

Place	Date	Hour	Summary of Events and Information	Remarks and references to Appendices
OOST DUNKERQUE BAINS	Feb 16th to 22nd		The Battalion carried out training and provided working parties daily for the line.	
	23rd		The Battalion relieved the 26th Battalion Royal Fusiliers in the left sub-sector of the Brigade front.	APPENDIX III
	24th to 25th		The Battalion occupied the left sub-sector of the Brigade front, A and D coys in the Front Line, C coy in Support and B Coy in Reserve. There were no casualties.	
	26th to 29th		The Battalion was relieved by the 10th Bn. Argyll and Sutherland Highlanders and proceeded to ST. IDESBALDE. A convoy of buses conveyed the Battalion from ST. IDESBALDE to the	APPENDIX IV

WAR DIARY
or
INTELLIGENCE SUMMARY

(Erase heading not required.)

Army Form C. 2118.

Place	Date	Hour	Summary of Events and Information	Remarks and references to Appendices
TETEGHEM	30th.		TETEGHEM AREA where billets were occupied. Route Marching and Training were carried out. A draft of 131. O.R. joined the Battalion.	
	31st.		Route marching and a Training were carried out under Battalion arrangements.	

R.W.Burn

LIEUT-COL.
KING'S ROYAL RIFLES,
COMMANDING 2nd BATTN.
(YEOMAN RIFLES)

SECRET.   Copy No. 8

124th. INFANTRY BRIGADE OPERATION ORDER NO. 157.

1.   The 124th. Infantry Brigade will relieve the 126th. Infantry Brigade in the Coast Defence Sector of the 41st Division Front on the 6th October under the following arrangements. Relief to be complete by 12 noon.

2.(a).   10th Bn. "Queens" R.W.S. Regt. will relieve the 1/5th East Lancashire Regt. in the Right Battalion Sector. Battalion Headquarters are at OOST DUNKERQUE BAINS R.27 d 8.2, where the head of the Battalion should arrive at 9.30 am.
Relief to be complete by 12 noon.
The Right Battalion Sector extends from EOLIAN Road R.24 c to about R.31 Central.

(b).   26th Bn. Royal Fusiliers will relieve the 1/9th Manchester Regt. in the Centre Battalion Sector, which extends from about R.31 Central to about W.10.c.
Battalion Headquarters are at COXYDE BAINS (W.6 a 5.4) where the head of the Battalion should arrive at 9.30 am.
Relief to be complete by 11.30 am.

(c).   21st Bn. K.R.R.C. will relieve the 1/10th Manchester Regt. in the Left Battalion Sector which extends from about W.10 c to the FRANCO-BELGIAN Boundary.
Battalion Headquarters are at LA PANNE BAINS (W.18 b 2.8) where the head of the Battalion should arrive at 9.30 am.
Relief to be complete by 11.30 am.

(d).   32nd Bn. Royal Fusiliers will relieve the 1/4th East Lancashire Regt. in the Reserve Battalion Sector.
Battalion Headquarters are at X.1 b Central (WILTSHIRE CAMP) where the head of the Battalion should arrive at 10 am. Relief to be complete by 11 am.

(e).   The 124th. Machine Gun Coy. will relieve the 126th Machine Gun Company placing 8 guns in position in the Brigade Sector.
The 124th. Machine Gun Coy. will also relieve 4 guns of the 126th Machine Gun Coy. which are lent to 125th. Infantry Brigade Machine Gun Coy. for the defence of the Front Sector.
The Company should arrive at the Machine Gun Coy. Headquarters (Q.31.d.) close to WILTSHIRE CAMP) at 9 am. following the 10th Bn. "Queens" R.W.S. Regt. on the march.

(f).   The 124th. L.T.M. Battery will relieve the 126th. L.T.M. Battery at WILTSHIRE CAMP (X.1 b Central) following the 32nd Bn. Royal Fusiliers on the march, and completing relief by 11 am.

3.   All details of relief to be arranged direct by Units concerned.
A motor bus will be at 124th. Infantry Brigade Headquarters GHYVELDE at 8.30 am. on the 5th instant to take Commanding Officers, Adjutants (and one or two other Officers if required) of Units to visit the Units they will be taking over from the next day.

4.   All maps, Defence Schemes, Trench Stores, etc. to be taken over on relief.

5.   124th. Infantry Brigade Headquarters will close at GHYVELDE at 11 am. on the 6th instant, and reopen at COXYDE BAINS (W.6 b 8.5) at the same hour.

                                                      Major,
                                                      Brigade Major,
                                                      124th. Infantry Brigade.

4/10/17.

Issued at 1.30 pm.

```
Copy No.  1   File.
 "   "    2   War Diary.
 "   "    3   41st Division G.
 "   "    4   126th. Infantry Brigade.
 "   "    5   10th Bn. "Queens" R.W.S. Regt.
 "   "    6   26th Bn. Royal Fusiliers.
 "   "    7   32nd Bn. Royal Fusiliers.
 "   "    8   21st Bn. K.R.R.C.
 "   "    9   124th. Machine Gun Coy.
 "   "   10   124th. Trench Mortar Battery.
 "   "   11   237th Field Coy. R.E.
 "   "   12   140th. Field Ambulance.
 "   "   13   No. 4 Coy. Divisional Train.
 "   "   14   Staff Captain.
 "   "   15   Brigade Signal Officer.
 "   "   16   Brigade Transport Officer.
```

SECRET.

ADMINISTRATIVE INSTRUCTIONS
Reference 124th. Infantry Brigade Order No.137.

1. ACCOMMODATION.
    On completion of relief the Division will be accommodated as shewn in attached Schedule.

2. S.A.A. - GRENADES.

    Divisional Dump is at R 33 b 2.0.
    Main Brigade Dump M 14 c 2.2.
    Additional Brigade Dump M 20 a 9.0.

    123rd. Infantry Brigade will detail an officer, 1 N.C.O. and 9 men to take charge of the Divisional Dump (until arrival of Divisional Artillery) on 5th. inst.

3. SUPPLIES.
    Supply Railhead changes to ST. IDESBALDE (Light Railway) W 17 b 5.5. on 7th. inst.

    Supply Refilling Point and Fuel Dumps will be at W 17 b 3.5.

4. WATER.
    There is no difficulty regarding water in this area, numerous water points and horse troughs exist.

5. ROADS & TRACKS.
    The two roads OOST DUNKERQUE BAINS - NIEUPORT BAINS and OOST DUNKERQUE - N 20 d are both fit for wheeled traffic by day as far E. as OOST DUNKERQUE - OOST DUNKERQUE BAINS Road, and by night to near Battalion H.Q. at M 19 b 1.9 and M 20 b 8.4.
    There are no tracks for transport.

6. TRAMWAYS.
    A map will be issued later showing Light Railways and Tramways in the Divisional Area.
    It is however more convenient under present circumstances to deliver both ammunition and rations by Horse Transport.

7. MEDICAL.
    A. D. S.   X 4 c 7.2.
              M 13 d 4.2.
    Ambulance H.Q. R 27 c 5.3.

8. R. E. STORES.
    Divisional Dump   X 8 d 3.8.
    Advanced Dumps No.1 R 23 d 4.4.
                   No.2 N 25 c 1.9.

9. COOKING.
    The Battalion in the Line use Trench Cookhouses. No Hot Food Containers yet available.

10. ORDNANCE.
    D.A.D.O.S. Store and Ordnance H.Q. is at W 10 d 8.8.

11. **VETERINARY.**
    No. 52nd. Mobile Veterinary Section will move to COXYDE BAINS in relief of No. 19 Mobile Veterinary Section, 42nd. Division on the 7th. inst.

12. **SALVAGE.**
    Dumps are situated -
    Main Divisional Dump   W 10 d 8.6.
    Brigade Dumps   X 1 a 2.9.
                            R 27 c 5.5.

    Divisional Salvage Officer will arrange with Salvage Officer 42nd. Division as to taking over.

13. **BATHS.**
    Divisional Baths are at ST. IDESBALDE.
    There are also some disused baths at OOST DUBKERQUE BAINS.
    Divisional Baths Officer will arrange with Divisional Baths Officer 42nd. Division to take over on 7th. instant.

14. **TRENCH STORES.**
    Battalions will render to this office by 6pm. on the 8th. inst. a return of:-
    (a) All trench stores taken over.
    (b) Total quantities of ammunition, fireworks, etc. in sector.
    (c) Locations of dumps, giving contents.

15. **ACKNOWLEDGE.**

P. M. Murray.
Captain,
Staff Captain,
124th. Infantry Brigade.

5/10/17.

Issued to all recipients of 124th. Inf. Bde.
Order No. 137.

SECRET.　　　　　　　　　　　　　　　　　　　　　　　124 I.B.
　　　　　　　　　　　　　　　　　　　　　　　　　　K.879.

Officer Commanding,
　　10th.Bn."Queens"
　　26th.Bn.R.Fusiliers.
　　32nd.Bn.R.Fusiliers.
　　21st.Bn.K.R.R.Corps.
　　124th.M.G.Coy.
　　124th.T.M.Bty.
　　237th.Field Coy.R.E.
　　No.4 Coy.Divl.Train.
　　Bde.Transport Officer.
　　Bde.Signal Officer.
　　140th.Field Ambulance.

　　　　Reference 124th.Infantry Brigade Order No.137
of 4/10/17.

1. **MOTOR TRANSPORT.**
　　　6 Motor Lorries will be available for carrying
blankets, etc. and are allotted as under:-
　　　Each Battalion.....1
　　　124th.M.G.Company)..1
　　　& 124th.T.M.Bty.　)
　　　Brigade Headqrs.....1

　　　The lorries will be at Brigade Headquarters,GHYVELDE,
at 8.30am. on the 6th.inst.　Units will send guides to
conduct lorries to their respective camps.
　　　Blankets, etc. should be stacked as near the main
road as possible as motor lorries are unable to get into
the camps by the sandy tracks.
　　　The lorry for the Machine Gun Coy. and Trench Mortar
Battery will proceed to the latter's Headquarters first.

2. **R. E. STORES.**
　　　The Divisional R. E. Dump in the new sector will be
MANCHESTER DUMP on road between COXYDE and OOST DUNKERKE
at X 8 d 3.8.
　　　The 237th.Field Company R.E.Dump will be at No.2
Advanced Dump at M 25 c 1.9.

3. **HANDING OVER CAMPS.**
　　　The camps occupied by Units of this Brigade Group will
be taken over by the Area Commandant this evening between
5pm. and 7pm.　The Staff Captain and Assistant Area
Commandant will visit all camps during the above times and
Units will have a statement prepared in duplicate giving
full particulars of numbers of huts, tents, Area Stores,
etc. to be handed over.

　　ACKNOWLEDGE.

　　　　　　　　　　　　　　　　　　P. M. Murray
　　　　　　　　　　　　　　　　　　　Captain,
　　　　　　　　　　　　　　　　　Staff Captain,
　　　　　　　　　　　　　　　124th. Infantry Brigade.

5/10/17.

SECRET.

LOCATION OF UNITS 41st. DIVISION.

Unit.	Location	Transport Lines.
Divisional H.Q.	ST. IDESBALDE	with unit
C. R. E.	"	"
41st. Signal Coy.	"	"
A.D.M.S.	"	"
D.A.D.V.S.	"	"
H.Q. Divl. Train		"
DAA.D.O.S.	W 10 d 8.8	
122nd Inf. Bde. H.Q.	W 10 d 7.3	W 10 d 5.3
1 Battalion	W 10 d 3.7	W 10 c 5.5
1 Battalion	W 11 c 3.6	W 11 c 2.7
1 Battalion	W 5 c 1.1	W 11 c 1.7
1 Battalion	W 10 b 4.7	W 10 d 3.7
122nd. M.G. Coy.	W 6 a 6.4	
122nd. T.M. Bty.	W 10 a 6.3	
124th. Inf. Bde. H.Q.	W 6 b 8.6	with unit
1 Battn.	X 1 b (Wiltshire Camp)	X 1 b 1.8
1 Battn.	R 27 d 80.20	R 33 a 4.2
1 Battn.	W 6 a 75.60	W 6 b 2.6
1 Battn.	LA PANNE	W 15 a 5.1
124th. M.G. Coy.	R 32 c 5.6	R 32 c 5.6
124th. T.M. Bty.	X 1 b (Wiltshire Camp)	
123rd. Inf. Bde. H.Q.	R 24 a 6.6 (Adv) R 33 d 7.9 (rear)	R 33 d 7.9
1 Battn.	M 19 b 1.9	R 32 b 8.3
1 Battn.	X 3 a 9.1	X 3 a 9.1
1 Battn.	R 27 c 3.3	R 32 b 8.3
1 Battn.	M 20 b 8.4	X 1 a 2.7
123rd. M.G. Coy.	R 24 a 3.5	
123rd. T.M. Bty.	R 32 b 2.4	
R. E.		
1 Field Company	R 32 a 5.0	R 31 d 6.5
1 Field Company	R 27 c 8.3	R 27 c 8.3
1 Field Company	M 15 a 7.3	R 27 c 6.2
R.A.M.C.		
1 Field Ambulance	X 25 b 7.8 (GROOTE KWINTE FARM)	with Unit
1 Field Ambulance	OOST DUNKERKE BAINS	"
1 Field Ambulance	ST. IDESBALDE	"
A.S.C.		
1 Company A.S.C.	W 18 c 5.9	with unit.
1 " "	W 18 a 2.5	"
1 " "	W 18 a 2.5	"
268th. Div. Emp. Coy.	ST. IDESBALDE.	
52nd. Mobile Vet. Sec.	COXYDE BAINS.	

APPENDIX I

OPERATION ORDER NO. 64.
by
MAJOR G. L. BROWN,
Commanding 21st Battalion King's Royal Rifle Corps.
Friday, 5th October, 1917.
----

1. The Battalion will relieve the 1/10th Manchesters in the Coast Defence Sector, W.9.d.9.9. on the East, to the Franco-Belgian Frontier on the West, V.23.d.3.5. to-morrow morning.

   Companies will be disposed as follows:-

   "A" Company, Right Sector from W.9.d.9.9. to W.13.d.5.4.
   "C"   "   "   "   " W.13.d.5.4. to left of Battalion
                                   Front V.23.d.3.5.

   "D" Company will be in close support to "A" Company and "B" Company in close support to "C" Company. "B" and "D" Companies will be billeted in LA PANNE BAINS.

   "A" Company's Sector will consist of 6 Posts. No. 1 to No. 6.
   "C"   "   "   "   "   "   3   "   No. 7 to No. 9.

   Details of these Posts as shown on attached form for defence.

   Six Guides of the 1/10th Manchesters will meet "A" Company on the beach opposite No. 6 Post, W.13.d.9.6. at 8-30 a.m.

   Three Guides will meet "C" Company on the beach at V.23.d.9.7. at 8-45 a.m.

   One Guide each for "B" and "D" Companies will be at Battalion Headquarters W.15.a.1.6. at 9-15 a.m.

   Companies will march independently leaving camp at the following times.

   "A" Company.   6-30 a.m.
   Headquarters and Signallers.   6-40 a.m.
   "C" Company.   6-50 a.m.
   "D"   "   7 a.m.
   "B"   "   7-10 a.m.

   Transport Lines will be at approximately W.15.a.5.3. They will proceed by road under the Quartermaster, leaving camp at 7-30 a.m.

2. All Company Baggage, Officers Valises and Mess Equipment will be ready for collection outside the Quartermasters Stores at 7 a.m. The Transport Officer will arrange to collect.

   All Blankets will be rolled in bundles of twenties and labelled and will be stacked at the entrance to the Camp near the Expeditionary Force Canteen. One man per Company will be detailed to look after these blankets, load them on the lorry and proceed with them to their destination.

   Headquarters Kit etc. will be outside Headquarters at 7 a.m.

   All Washing Bowls will be sent to the Quartermasters Stores before 7 a.m.

   O.C. Companies are responsible that their camps are left scrupulously clean.

   G L Brown
                                     Major.
                        Commanding 21st Bn. K.R.R.C.

No. 1 Post.   1 Section.
 " 2 "   2 Sections with 2 Lewis Guns.
 " 3 "   2 Sections " 3 "   "
Battalion O.P. & Signallers.
No. 4 Post.   3 Sections.
 " 5 "   2   "
 " 6 "   2 Lewis Gun Sections.
 " 7. "   3 Sections.
 " 8 "   1 Platoon and 1 Lewis Gun Section.
 " 9. "   1 Platoon.

Owing to the shortage of Lewis Guns the Lewis Gun Officer will arrange for "B" and "D" Companies to lend their Lewis Guns to the Companies on the defensive if necessary.

SECRET.  Copy No. 9

124th. INFANTRY BRIGADE OPERATION ORDER NO. 138.

1. The 124th. Infantry Brigade will be relieved in the Coast Defence Sector by the 122nd. Infantry Brigade on the 15th instant, and on completion of this relief, will relieve the 123rd. Infantry Brigade in the NIEUPORT BAINS Sector under the following arrangements.-

2. (a) The 10th Bn. "Queens" R.W.S. Regt. will be relieved by the 12th Bn. E. Surrey Regt. in the Right Battalion Sector. The head of the relieving Battalion will be at Battalion Headquarters, OOST-DUNKERKE-BAINS at 10.30 am. on the 15th instant, and relief must be complete by 1 pm.

(b) The 10th Bn. "Queens" R.W.S. Regt. will, on relief, move to and take over the Camp at YORKSHIRE CAMP (X.3.a.9.4.) from 10th Bn. R.W. Kents. They will arrive at YORKSHIRE CAMP at 2 pm. and relief must be complete by 2.30 pm.

3. (a) 26th Bn. Royal Fusiliers will be relieved in the Centre battalion Sector by the 11th R.W. Kents, the head of whose column will arrive at Battalion Headquarters, COXYDE BAINS, at 12.30 pm. on the 15th instant. Relief should be complete by 2 pm.

(b) 26th Bn. Royal Fusiliers will relieve the 23rd. Bn. Middlesex Regt. and 1 Company of the 20th D.L.I. in the Left Battalion Sector of the Front Line. The head of the Battalion should arrive at the Cross Roads OOST-DUNKERKE-BAINS at 5.15 pm. where guides from the 23rd.Bn.Middlesex Regt. will meet it. Battalion Headquarters of the Left Battalion in the Line is at M.19 a 2.9.

4. (a) The 21st Bn. K.R.R.C. will be relieved in the Left Battalion Sector by the 18th Bn. K.R.R.C., the head of whose column will be at Battalion Headquarters, LA PANNE at 9.30 am. Relief should be complete by 11 am.

(b) 21st Bn. K.R.R.C. will, on relief, march to MIDDLESEX CAMP (R.27.c.3.3.) to relieve the 20th Bn. D.L.I.. The head of the column should arrive at MIDDLESEX CAMP at 1 pm. and relief should be complete by 1.30 pm.

5. (a) 32nd Bn. Royal Fusiliers will be relieved in the Reserve Battalion Sector by the 15th Bn. Hampshire Regt., the head of whose column will be at WILTSHIRE CAMP at 3 pm. Relief should be complete by 3.30 pm.

(b) 32nd Bn. Royal Fusiliers will relieve the 11th Bn. "Queens" in the Right Battalion Sector of the Front Line. The head of the column should arrive at the Road Junction OOST-DUNKERKE (X.4 c 4.4) at 5.15 pm. where they will be met by guides of the 11th Bn. "Queens". The Headquarters of the Right Battalion in the Line is at the Cross Roads M.20 b 8.4.

6. (a) The 122nd. Machine Gun Coy. will relieve the 124th.Machine Gun Coy. in the Coast Defence Sector on the 14th instant, under arrangements to be made between Company Commanders concerned; relief to be complete by 1 pm.

(2).

6.(b). The 124th. Machine Gun Coy. will relieve the 123rd. Machine Gun Coy. in the line on the 14th and night 14th/15th instant, under arrangements to be made between Company Commanders concerned; relief to be complete by midnight. As many guns as possible should be relieved during daylight.

Four guns of the 122nd. Machine Gun Coy. are being lent to the 124th. Machine Gun Coy. and will proceed with them on relief.

7.(a) The 122nd.L.T.M.Battery will relieve the 124th.L.T.M.Battery on the 14th instant under arrangements to be made between Battery Commanders concerned. The 122nd.L.T.M.Battery will arrive at WILTSHIRE CAMP at 2.30 pm. and relief should be complete by 3 pm.

(b) The 124th. L.T.M.Battery will relieve the 123rd.L.T.M.Battery in the Line on the night 14th/15th instant, under arrangements to be made between Battery Commanders concerned; relief to be complete by midnight.

8. One Officer per Battalion, one Officer, one N.C.O. and 2 Runners per Company, One Officer per Machine Gun Coy and L.T.M.Battery with one N.C.O. per Section and one man per gun, of the Units proceeding to the line, will be sent forward 24 hours previous to relief to live with their opposite numbers. They should be at the Cross Roads OOST-DUNKERKE-BAINS at 10 am. on the 13th or 14th instant as the case may be, where arrangements have been made for guides to meet them.

9. All further details of relief will be arranged between Unit Commanders concerned.
Representatives from Units proceeding to the line to fix these further details should be at OOST-DUNKERKE-BAINS Cross Roads at 9 am. on the 13th instant, where a guide will meet them and take them to Brigade Headquarters, and further guides thence to Unit Headquarters.

10. All maps, defence schemes, trench stores, etc. will be handed and taken over on relief.

11. The usual intervals as laid down in this Office G.74 dated 30/9/17 will be observed on the march.

12. 124th.Infantry Brigade Headquarters will close at COXYDE BAINS at 7 am. on the 16th instant and will open at OOST DUNKERKE (Advance Headquarters NIEUPORT BAINS) at the same hour.

13. Completion of relief will be reported to this Office by wire using the name of the Commanding Officer followed by the time.

14. ACKNOWLEDGE.

Major,
Brigade Major,
124th.Infantry Brigade.

12/10/17.

Issued at 8.30 pm.

Copy No. 1   File.
"   "   2   War Diary.
"   "   3   41st Division G.
"   "   4   122nd. Infantry Brigade.
"   "   5   123rd. Infantry Brigade.
"   "   6   10th Bn. "Queens" R.W.S.Regt.
"   "   7   26th Bn. Royal Fusiliers.
"   "   8   32nd Bn. Royal Fusiliers.
"   "   9   21st Bn. K.R.R.C.
"   "   10   124th. Machine Gun Coy.
"   "   11   124th. L.T.M.Battery.
"   "   12   Staff Captain.
"   "   13   Brigade Transport Officer.
"   "   14   Brigade Signal Officer.

SECRET.

ORDERLY ROOM
Date 13·10·17
No. K160
21st K.R.R. (YEOMAN RIFLES)

124 I.B.
K.901

To:- Officer Commanding,
    10th Bn. "Queens" R.W.S.Regt.
    26th Bn. Royal Fusiliers.
    32nd Bn. Royal Fusiliers.
    21st Bn. K.R.R.C.

    With reference to 124th Infantry Brigade Operation Order No. 138, battalions in the front line will only take in with them 550 all ranks (including Battalion Headquarters), the remainder of the battalion being left at YORKSHIRE and MIDDLESEX CAMPS. The Left Battalion in the Line will in addition to the 350 accommodate 125 men in tunnels in the Reserve Line M.19 b 6.9, for work under the R.E.

12/10/17.

                          Major,
                      Brigade Major,
               124th Infantry Brigade.

SECRET. Copy No. 9

AMENDMENT TO 124th. INFANTRY BRIGADE OPERATION ORDER NO. 138.
****

124th. Infantry Brigade Headquarters will close at COXYDE BAINS at 4 p.m. on 15th instant, and open at OOST DUNKERKE (Advanced Headquarters NIEUPORT BAINS) at the same hour.

C.C. Ling.
Major,
Brigade Major,
124th. Infantry Brigade.

13/10/17.

Issued to all recipients of 124th. Infantry Brigade Operation Order No. 138.

APPENDIX II

Copy No. 15.

OPERATION ORDER NO. 65.
by
LIEUT.-COL. G. L. BROWN.
Commanding 21st Battalion King's Royal Rifle Corps.
Saturday, 13th October, 1917.

----

1. The Battalion will be relieved by the 18th Bn. K.R.R.C. 122nd Infantry Brigade in the LA PANNE Coast Defence Sector on Monday the 15th instant.
   Relief to be completed by 11 a.m.

2. O.C. "D" Company will arrange to have one guide from each Post on the beach opposite No. 6 Post at 9-15 a.m. to meet "D" Company, 18th Bn. K.R.R.C. and guide them into their positions.

   O.C. "B" Company will arrange to have one guide per Post on the beach opposite No. 9 Post at 9 a.m. to meet "B" Company, 18th Bn. K.R.R.C. and guide them into their positions.

   Headquarters, "A" and "C" Companies will each have one guide on the beach opposite Battalion Headquarters at 9-30 a.m. to guide their respective units of the 18th Bn. K.R.R.C. into the billets occupied by them.

   The Battalion O.P. and all Signalling arrangements will be handed over under the supervision of the Signal Officer.

3. Relief will be reported correct by the Company Commanders name and time.

4. All Defence Scheme Maps etc. will be handed over to the incoming unit.

5. On relief the Battalion will move to MIDDLESEX CAMP, R.27.c.3.3. and will relieve the 20th Bn. D.L.I. leaving LA PANNE as follows:-

Headquarters and Band.	10-20 a.m.
"A" Company.	10-30 a.m.
"C" "	10-40 a.m.
"D" "	10-50 a.m.
"B" "	11 a.m.

   Transport will move to MIDDLESEX CAMP under the Transport Officer as soon as relief is complete.

6. <u>Baggage</u>. All Officers Valises, Company Baggage and Mess Boxes of "D", "A" and "C" Companies will be ready for collection at 9-30 a.m. outside their respective Headquarters - "B" Company at 9 a.m.

   The Transport Officer will arrange to collect.

   Details for the conveyance of Blankets will be issued later.

7. <u>Stores</u>. All billets stores and stores for the improvement of billets will be handed over to the incoming unit.

P.F. Smith

2nd Lieut.
A/Adjutant.
21st Bn. K.R.R.C.

Issued at... 10 p.m.

Distribution.

Copy No. 1. Commanding Officer.
2. Second in Command.
3. O.C. "A" Company.
4. " "B" "
5. " "C" "
6. " "D" "
7. Transport Officer.
8. Quartermaster.
9. Signal Officer.
10. 20th Bn. D.L.I.
11. 16th Bn. K.R.R.C.
12. R.S.M.
13. War Diary.
14. File.
15. Spare.

SECRET.

Officer Commanding,
    10th. Bn. "Queens" R.W.S.
    26th. Bn. R. Fusiliers.
    32nd. Bn. R. Fusiliers.
    21st. Bn. K.R.R. Corps.   Area Commandant COXYDE BAINS
    124th. M.G. Coy.   Area Commandant OOST DUNKERKE BAINS
    124th. T.M. Bty.   Staff Captain.
    41st. Division G.
    122nd. Inf. Bde.
    123rd. Inf. Bde.
    Bde. Signal Officer
    Bde. Transport Officer

121 I.B.
K.906

        With reference to 124th. Infantry Brigade Order No.138 of 12th. inst.

1. <u>TRANSPORT.</u>
        The following is the disposition of Units Transport on and after the 15th. inst.

    10th. Bn. "Queens" R.W.S.   On the COXYDE-COXYDE BAINS road at X 1 c 3.1.

    26th. Bn. R. Fusiliers   Will take over from the 10th. R.W. Kents at X 1 a 2.8.

    32nd. Bn. R. Fusiliers   On the COXYDE-COXYDE BAINS Road at X 1 c 3.1.

    21st. Bn. K.R.R. Corps   Will take over from the 23rd. Bn. Middlesex Regt. at R 32 b 3.2.

    124th. M.G. Coy.   Will take over from the 123rd. M.G. Coy.

    Brigade Headquarters   In KENT CAMP at R 33 c 7.5.

    All transport will move under arrangements to be made by Os.C. Units.

2. <u>DETAILS.</u>
    The details of the 26th. Bn. R. Fusiliers and 32nd. Bn. R. Fuslrs. will be accommodated in KENT CAMP. (R 33 c 7.5)
    The 26th. Bn. R. Fusiliers will detail 1 N.C.O., and the 32nd. R. Fusiliers 2 N.C.Os. to report to the Area Commandant, OOST-DUNKERKE BAINS (R 27 c 65.45) at 9 am, tomorrow 15th. inst. These N.C.Os. will take with them full particulars as to accommodation required for officers and Other Ranks of their respective Units and will be allotted huts for these by the Area Commandant.

    ACKNOWLEDGE.

                                    P.M. Murray
                                        Captain,
                                    Staff Captain,
                            124th. Infantry Brigade.

14/10/17.

Copy No. 11.

APPENDIX III

OPERATION ORDER NO. 66.
by
LIEUT.-COL. G. L. BROWN.
Commanding 21st Battalion King's Royal Rifle Corps.
Sunday, 21st October, 1917.

1. The Battalion will relieve "Drop" on the night of the 23/24th October, 1917, and will be disposed as follows:-

   Right Front.   "Hare".
   Left Front.   "Fox".
   Support.   "Bird".
   Reserve.   "Stag".

2. LEWIS GUNS.

   (a). The Lewis Gun Officer will arrange for 7 Lewis Gun Teams complete with guns and 20 drums per section, to relieve the front line posts at dawn on the 23rd. Guides from "Drop" will meet them at 5 a.m. where BATH ALLEY cuts BATH AVENUE.

   (b). 5 Lewis Gun Teams from "Drop" will after relief meet the Lewis Gun Officer at 10 a.m. where BATH ALLEY cuts BATH AVENUE to relieve our Aeroplane posts.

   (c). 3 Teams of Lewis Gunners after relief from the Aeroplane Posts will take over 3 Posts in the Support Line from "Drop". Guides will meet the Lewis Gun Officer at the junction of BUTCHER ALLEY and BATH AVENUE at 3 p.m.

   (d). All adjustments to get Company teams together will be made as soon as possible on the morning of the 24th. Teams not used in the line will be held in reserve with Company Headquarters.

3. COMMUNICATIONS.

   The Signal Officer will arrange to have 4 Signallers for Battalion Headquarters and 2 Signallers for each Company to report at Battalion Headquarters "Drop" at 12 noon on the 23rd. The remainder of the Signallers will move with their Companies and Headquarters respectively.

4. O.C. "Fox" will arrange for 6 men to report with Lewis Gunners at 5 a.m. on the 23rd to occupy 3 Pom-pom Posts. Teams for these posts should not consist of more than 1 N.C.O. and 3 men for each gun.

5. The Sniping Sergeant will detail 4 men, 1 to each post to be taken over and will report to Headquarters, "Drop", at 12 noon on the 23rd.

6. The order of relief will be as follows:-

   1 "Hare".
   2 "Fox". 3 "Bird".
   4 "Stag".
   5 "Headquarters".

   Starting Point. Battalion Orderly Room.

   Route:- OOST DUNKERKE BAINS, WIRE TRACK, BATH AVENUE. Platoons at not less than 300 yards interval.

   Time to be notified later.

   Guides from "Drop" will meet these Companies at the junction of BATH AVENUE and BUTCHER ALLEY.

Dress:- Full Marching Order, Great Coat and Blanket to be carried in pack.

2 Sandbags per Section, for Caps and Small Kit will be left behind at the Transport. These will be clearly labelled shewing the Company and Section and should be dumped by Companies at the Transport Lines not later than 3 p.m. on the 23rd.

The Transport Officer will make arrangements for this.

7. RATIONS.

Rations will be delivered nightly at Battalion Headquarters and will be delivered by "Bird" to Front Line Company Headquarters. C.Q.M.Sergeants will accompany rations and will personally hand them over to the Officers Commanding their Companies.

8. WATER.

O.C. "Bird" will attach 6 men to "Hare" for Water Duties.

9. O.C. "Bird" will detail 20 men daily to report to the permanent Medical Officer at 9 a.m.

10. 1 N.C.O. and 3 men on Traffic Control at the LAITERIE will on being relieved by "Drop" proceed to the line and report to Battalion Headquarters.

11. All Defence Schemes, Maps and Trench Stores will be taken over on relief.

12. Relief will be reported complete by the code name followed by time.

P. F. Smith.
Capt.
Adjutant.
21st Bn. K.R.R.C.

Issued at 3 p.m.

Copy No. 1. Commanding Officer.
      2. Second in Command.
      3. O.C. "Hare".
      4. "   "Stag".
      5. "   "Bird".
      6. "   "Fox".
      7. Transport Officer.
      8. Quartermaster.
      9. Signal Officer.
    10. Lewis Gun Officer.
    11. War Diary.
    12. R.S.M.
    13. File.
    14. "DROP" (for information)

SECRET.   Copy No. 10

124th. INFANTRY BRIGADE ORDER
No. 139.

1.   The 10th. Bn. "Queens" R.W.S. will relieve the 32nd. Bn. Royal Fusiliers in the Right Battalion sub-sector, and the 21st. Bn. K.R.R. Corps will relieve the 26th. Bn. Royal Fusiliers in the left Battalion sub-sector of the Brigade Front on the night 23rd/24th. October, under detailed arrangements to be made between Battalion Commanders concerned.
     Relief to be complete by 5 am. on 24th. inst.

2.   All Trench maps, Defence Schemes, programmes of work, trench stores, etc. are to be handed over on relief.

3.   Completion of relief to be notified to this office by the name of the Commanding Officer followed by the time.

                                       for Major,
                                       Brigade Major,
22/10/17.   124th. Infantry Brigade.

          Issued to Signals at 1.15pm.

          Copy No. 1   File
            "   2   War Diary
            "   3   41st. Div. G.
            "   4   127th. Inf. Bde.
            "   5   122nd. Inf. Bde.
            "   6   123rd. Inf. Bde.
            "   7   10th. Bn. "Queens"
            "   8   26th. Bn. R. Fuslrs.
            "   9   32nd. Bn. R. Fuslrs.
            "   10   21st. Bn. K.R.R.C.
            "   11   124th. M.G. Coy.
            "   12   124th. T.M. Bty.
            "   13   Staff Captain.
            "   14   Bde. Signal Officer.
            "   15   Bde. Transport Officer.

Y.R.C. 26.

ADDENDA to OPERATION ORDER NO. 66.
----

1. Guides from "Drop" will be at the junction of BATH AVENUE and BATH ALLEY at 5-45 p.m. to-morrow 23rd instant.
   O.C. "Hare" will arrange for the head of his Company to reach this point at that hour.

2. Camp Kettles will be taken up with rations. They should be dumped at the Quartermasters Stores with the rations to-morrow afternoon.

3. The R.S.M. and Company Sergeant Majors will be at Headquarters "Drop" at 12 noon to-morrow.

4. The Provost Sergeant will report at Battalion Headquarters "Drop" at 10 a.m. to-morrow.

5. The Medical Officer's Orderly will report to the Medical Officer in the line at 12 noon to-morrow.

6. The Sections Bags and Officers Surplus Kit will be dumped at the Quartermasters Stores and <u>not</u> at the Transport.

7. The attention of Company Commanders is drawn to their responsibility in the taking over of stores. They will sign for the stores taken over, and before doing so must ensure that they have been checked by the Company Sergeant Major.
   A list of stores taken over will be forwarded to the Battalion Orderly Room by 10 a.m. on the 24th instant.

Issued at 6 p.m.

To all recipients of Operation Order No. 66.

                                                              Capt.
                                                            Adjutant.

22-10-17.   21st Bn. K.R.R.C.

Secret   Copy No.

124th Infantry Brigade Orders No. 141.

(1) 124th Inf. Bde. Warning Order No. 13 dated 28/10/17 is confirmed.

(2) 124th Inf. Bde. will be relieved by 126th Inf. Bde. in accordance with attached table.

(3) On relief Units will move to embussing point under instructions which will be issued by the Staff Captain.

(4) Defence Schemes, Trench Maps, Aerophotos, programmes of work, trench stores, etc. will be handed over on relief.

(5) The usual intervals as laid down in this Office G.7 dated 30/9/17 will be observed on the march.

(6) (a) During the journey by bus, a sentry and a detachment with loaded rifles will be posted on the top of each bus to watch for hostile aircraft.

(b) A similar look-out will also be maintained by troops in lorries.

(c) In case of attack by hostile aircraft, the busses will halt and troops will scatter off the road and bring fire to bear upon the E.A.

(7) Completion of relief will be reported to this Office by wire, the name of the Commanding Officer followed by the hour.

(8) Command will pass from G.O.C. 124th Inf. Bde. to G.O.C. 26th Inf. Bde. at 10 pm. 28th Oct.

(9) Position of Brigade Headquarters on relief will be notified later.

(10) Acknowledge.

W.B.Hawthorn...........
Capt.
a/ Bde Major
124th Inf. Bde.

28/10/17
Issued to Signals at 3.55 pm.

Copy No. 1 File
2 War Diary
3 4th Div.
4 122nd Bde
5 26th Inf Bde
6 10th Queen's
7 26th R.Fus.
8 32nd R.Fus.
9 21st KRRC

Copy No. 10 124th M.G. Coy
11. 124th LTM Bty
12. 233rd Fd Coy
13. Staff Capt.
14. Bde Sy Officer
15. Bde Class
16. Spare

APPENDIX IV

OPERATION ORDER NO. 67.
by
LIEUT.-COL. G. L. BROWN.
Commanding 21st Battalion King's Royal Rifle Corps.
Sunday, 28th October, 1917.

1. The Battalion will be relieved in the line this evening by the 10th Argyll and Sutherland Highlanders.

2. Three guides per Company (1 per Platoon) will be at the cross roads OOST DUNKERKE BAINS at 5-15 p.m.

3. The Companies of the relieving Battalion will be disposed as follows:-

    Left Front.   "D".
    Right Front.   "B".
    Support.   "A".
    Reserve.   "C".

4. Officers Trench Bundles, Mess Equipment and Company Cooking utensils will be dumped at Battalion Headquarters by 6-30 p.m.

5. On being relieved Companies will proceed to a convoy of buses on the COXYDE BAINS - IDESBALDE ROAD.

6. The Model Platoon will join "B" Company and the Band will join Headquarters at MIDDLESEX CAMP.

7. Three men per bus will be posted on top as Aeroplane Guards.

8. All Trench Maps, Defence Schemes etc. will be handed over on relief.

9. Relief will be reported to Battalion Headquarters using Code name and time.

P. F. Smith
Capt.
Adjutant.
21st Bn. K.R.R.C.

Issued at 3-30 p.m.

Copy No. 1. Commanding Officer.
        2. 2nd in Command.
        3. Adjutant.
        4. Hare.
        5. Stag.
        6. Bird.
        7. Fox.
        8. Transport Officer.
        9. Quartermaster.
       10. War Diary.
       11. R.S.M.
       12. File.

124th INF. BDE.

Serial No	Unit of 124th Inf Bde to be relieved & location	By unit of 26th Inf Bde	Guides 1 per section at 1 pm Batt H.Q. at	at time	Reinf to complete by	Entraining Point	Destination
1.	3/4th Bn. K.E.R.C. (Right S.L. Sector)	10th A&S. Highlanders	OOST DUNKERKE BRINT R.27.C.60.90.	5.15 pm	9 pm 28th	COXYDE - COXYDE BAINS - ST IDESBALDE TOUR	TETEGHEM AREA
2.	10th Queens R.W.S. (Right Sub Sector)	5th/7th Black Watch	OOST DUNKERKE R.27.C.40.40.	10.30 pm	5 a.m. 29th	do.	do.
3.	24th R. Fus. (3 Coys in support J Res.)	5th Cameron Highlanders	OOST DUNKERKE BAINS R.27.C.60.90.	12.30 am	5 a.m. 29th	do.	do.
4.	124th M.G. Coy.	26th M.G. Coy.	Under arrangements to be made between C.Os concerned		5 a.m. 29th	do.	do.
5.	124th L.T.M. Bty.	26th L.T.M. Bty.			5 a.m. 29th	do.	do.
6.	32nd R.F. (Reserve)	7/Lafork Highrs	at Yorkshire C.		9 p.m. 28th	do.	do.